contents

Candle making is a relatively simple craft with its origins firmly grounded in ancient history. The necessary materials and equipment are readily available from craft and specialist shops everywhere, in fact, you will probably find that you already possess most of the basic equipment in your kitchen at home. So, armed with this book, there is nothing to stop you exploring this creative and satisfying craft.

Candle making requires a heat source, therefore the obvious place to make candles is in the kitchen. But do take heed, the craft is quite addictive and absorbing, as my poor parents will confirm. They paid me a brief visit while I was in the midst of the experimentation and preparation of the projects in this book. My kitchen was strictly a candles only, no-cook zone, with hubbling, bubbling pans of molten wax on the stove and projects in various stages of completion balanced precariously on every available surface. "We'll go out for dinner then?" they suggested hopefully, with absolutely no arguments from me.

This book falls basically into two parts. First you will find an information and techniques section, followed by a series of 21 inspirational projects. The former provides comprehensive, illustrated details on the basic and more specialized equipment and materials you are likely to need, detailing the use and application of each.

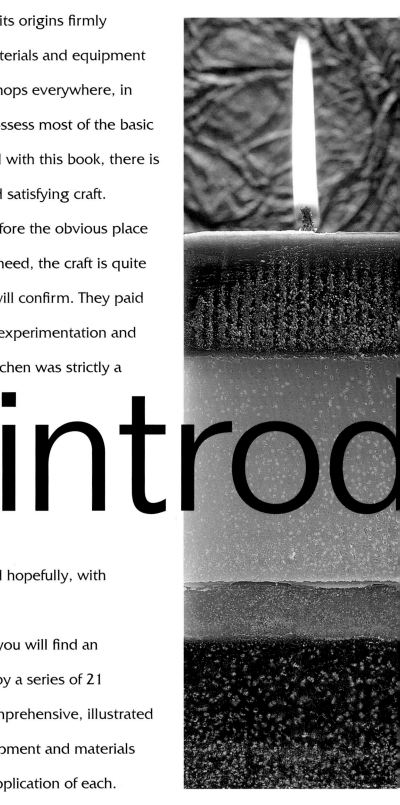

introd

The basic techniques of candle making and some special effects are also described. By reading carefully through this section you will be able to confidently complete all the projects that follow.

It is by no means necessary to gather all the equipment at once, instead it is advisable, if you are a complete beginner, to buy simply the bare essentials. Then, if the candle-making bug bites, you can think about buying more expensive and varied materials and moulds.

The projects chosen for this book are intended to both instruct and inspire, and are designed as a practical starting point for candle making. Why not try your own combination of techniques and colours for spectacular effects? And don't forget, wax can always be remelted and reused, so don't despair if your early attempts are somewhat disappointing.

The joy of any new craft is being able to use basic, new-found skills together with your imagination and artistic style to create unique projects that are both useful and decorative, and reflect a part of you. I am sure you will discover, as I have, that candle making is a wonderful and enjoyable way to express your own individuality, and is also far more satisfying than buying ready-made, mass-produced candles from a shop. I hope you will enjoy this book and will continue to enjoy making and using candles as a part of your life.

a brief history of candle making

How fortunate we are today to be able to illuminate darkness with the mere flick of a switch. The luxury of instant, artificial light, however, is a fairly recent one. No more than 150 years ago the humble candle, together with oil lamps, were the only source of artificial light available. And yet, even though electricity and gas are now the common power sources in most homes, we still choose to use candles, no longer out of necessity but for the sheer irresistible charm of a flickering flame.

The basic methods of candle making remain the same as in centuries past. Essentially, a candle is a cylinder of solid fuel with a central wick. Traditionally, most candles for domestic use were made out of tallow, a substance obtained from animal fat, and wicks were made from rush or flax. However, tallow would smell revolting when burning, and rush or flax wicks smoked terribly. The only alternative material available for candle making was beeswax, which, due to its costliness, was reserved for use by the very wealthy and the church. And even then, because of the quality of the wicks, the candles very often did not burn evenly.

In the early nineteenth century, due to the research and experimentation of a French chemist called Michael Chevreul, it was discovered that a substance called stearin could be separated from tallow. Stearin could be used to harden other fats, giving rise to the production of cheaper, odour-free, better quality candles. As the century progressed, petroleum oil and coal began to be used increasingly as energy sources. A by-product of this industry was the extraction of paraffin wax.

These two basic ingredients, stearin and paraffin wax, transformed the burning quality of candles, and, with the exception of beeswax, replaced all other substances used in the candle-making process. They remain the principal

ingredients today, though stearin is now made from palm nuts, and paraffin wax is a by-product of refining petrol.

Another great advance, which took place during the same period, was the introduction of plaited wicks. Rush and flax wicks caused candles to burn unevenly and smoke and made it necessary to snuff and trim the wick at regular intervals. Experimentation with different materials resulted, in 1825, with another Frenchman, M. Cambaceres, producing a wick made from plaited cotton threads, which was found to give a brighter, more constant flame. There still remained, however, the problem of the ash which was produced by the braided cotton. It was eventually discovered that if wicks were soaked in boric acid they became self-consuming when lit. Coincidentally, it was just at that time, when candle making was finally perfected, that the use of electricity as a source of lighting became viable and widespread.

Today, the use of candles is enjoying a revival, and candle makers have access to a vast array of wax products, moulds and decorative materials with which to experiment. The projects in this book employ a range of simple techniques, which, it is hoped, will instruct and inspire the reader to create beautiful original candles to keep for pleasure or to give as a gift.

necessities

Candle-making techniques require a number of pieces of necessary equipment, some of which you will probably already find in the kitchen or home study. For the majority of projects described in this book, you will need a double boiler and a thermometer, a wicking needle and suitable wick support, a craft knife, a baking tray, a water bath, and sometimes weights, and a mould and mould sealer. Any additional equipment is specified in the individual projects.

ADHESIVE TAPES: Double-sided adhesive tape is used in the construction of card moulds which are then sealed on the outside with packing tape. Strips of masking tape are used to mark the level a mould should be filled up to when making striped candles.

BAKING TRAY: It is often a good idea to put candle moulds on a baking tray, to catch any wax leakage, and seal them in place with mould sealer.

BRADAWL: This tool is used to pierce a hole in a "found" mould, such as a plastic or cardboard food container, to thread the wick through.

CARD AND CARD TUBES: Sheets of stiff card are useful for making your own candle moulds, especially shiny card which does not stick to the wax. Ready-made card tubes can also be used as pillar moulds. Card food containers can also be easily adapted into candle moulds.

CRAFT KNIFE: A sharp craft knife is an invaluable tool for the candle maker in a multitude of ways, including its uses for simple wick trimming, cutting beeswax sheets to size and cutting card moulds from templates.

DIPPING CAN: A tall, metal, cylindrical vessel is necessary for holding molten wax when making long,

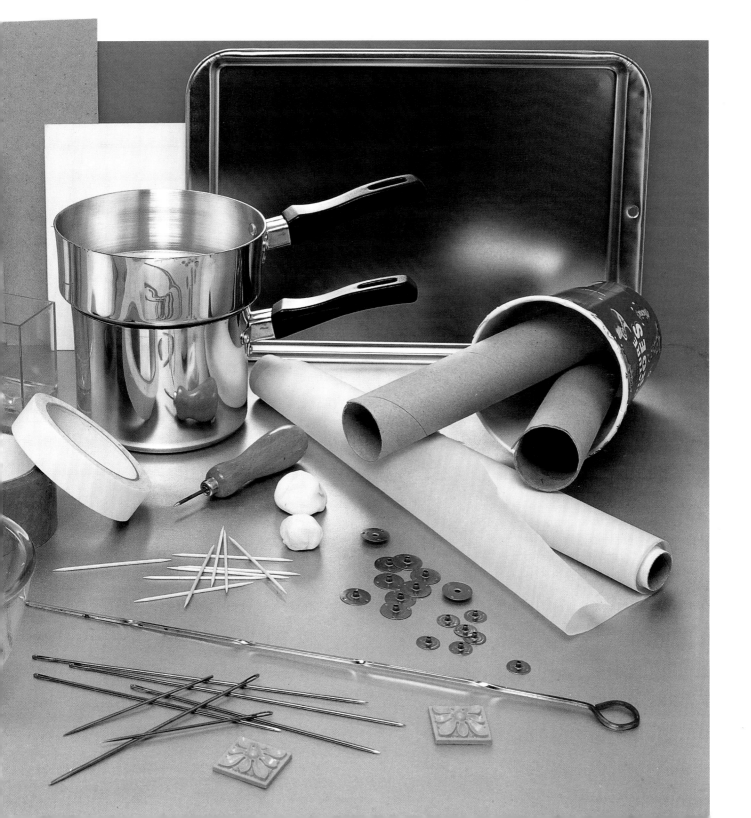

hand-dipped candles, and for the crackled pyramid project (see pages 46–47). Dipping cans are available in a variety of sizes, depending on the size of the candle required. As they are a specialized and costly piece of equipment, you could use a tall metal food can instead.

DOUBLE BOILER: The double boiler is an essential piece of equipment in candle making, and should be made from either aluminium or stainless steel. Wax begins to vapourize when it overheats, and can then easily catch fire, therefore, the safest way to heat it is over water. Put the wax in the upper pan, and water in the lower one. Then bring the water to the boil and leave it to simmer while the wax melts. Care must be taken not to let the lower pan boil dry, so remember to top it up regularly.

EMBOSSING MOULDS: Small, plastic decorative mouldings can be bought to emboss candles. They are glued to the inside of cardboard moulds using waterproof glue. Alternatively, cut out your own shapes from stiff card and use these in the same way.

GLASS BOWLS: It is always advisable to have a few small glass containers close at hand, for weighing wax, using as water baths or for storing small amounts of leftover wax for use at a later date.

GREASEPROOF PAPER: This waxy paper is useful for lining glass containers used to hold leftover wax. It can also be dipped into stearin or wax while colouring it to check the approximate dried shade.

HEAT SOURCE: Candle making is a craft that can be carried out in the kitchen, using either a gas or electric hob. However, a small camping stove is useful if you have a separate work room.

KITCHEN TOWEL: No candle maker should be without a roll of kitchen towel within easy reach, to mop up spills, clean thermometers, protect moulds and to generally keep the work area clean.

METAL SKEWER: A metal skewer is a useful implement for stirring molten wax or stearin, and can be wiped clean with a kitchen towel. Do not leave the skewer in the hot mixture and wear oven gloves to protect your hands.

MOULDS: There are a number of ready-made moulds available to buy (see page 14), or you can make your own using cardboard or clean "found" hollow objects such as plastic or cardboard food containers, glass jars or salad bowls (see pages 20–21).

MOULD SEALER: This candle-making product is a sticky, putty-like, non-setting mastic that is waterproof and reusable. It is primarily used to seal around the wick and wick hole of a mould, to prevent wax leaking out, It can also be used to fix the base of card moulds to the baking tray, again to prevent wax seepage. The importance of using a good mould sealer cannot be stressed enough.

PLAIN PAPER: Sheets of plain paper are useful to have around when tracing out templates.

RULER: A metal ruler can be used to shape a candle made from rolled beeswax sheets, and is also useful when scoring lines to help fold a card mould.

SPOON: A wooden or metal spoon is useful for mixing wax, stearin and dyes together in the double boiler. Wax dye should be crushed with the back of a metal spoon before it is added to molten stearin or wax.

THERMOMETER: Temperature control is a crucial element of the candle-making process, as the quality and nature of the finished product often depends on careful monitoring of the temperature and pouring just at the right moment. The thermometer should be able to measure temperatures between about 38°C (100°F) and 121°C (250°F). Always wipe it clean with a piece of kitchen towel when you remove it from the wax. You could use a specialist wax thermometer from candle-making suppliers, or a sugar thermometer.

TRACING PAPER: Keep this transparent paper handy when making your own moulds using the templates in this book (see pages 76–77).

WATER BATH AND WEIGHTS: Any container that the mould can sit in and be surrounded by water can be used as a water bath to speed up the wax setting time. Old-fashioned kitchen weights or pebbles can be used to hold down a rigid mould.

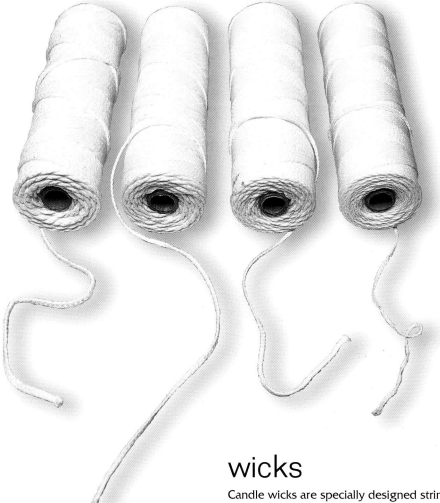

wicks

Candle wicks are specially designed strings of plaited cotton treated with boric acid. They are available in various thicknesses for use with candles of different diameters and widths. It is extremely important to choose the correct size of wick for each candle. If the wick is too large, it will provide too much heat, and the candle may smoke and wax drip down the outside. If the wick is too small, on the other hand, it will burn down in a cavity in the centre of the candle, causing the candle flame to become drowned in molten wax.

Professional candle makers classify a wick by the number of strands it contains, but, as the size of the wick required is determined by the diameter or width of the candle you are making, most people simply ask their suppliers for this measurement. For example, for a 5 cm (2 in) candle you would ask for a 5 cm (2 in) wick. This will burn with a pool of wax that reaches just to the outside of the candle.

WICKING NEEDLE: These sturdy needles are used for threading wicks into moulds and piercing holes in cardboard moulds. They are available in a variety of sizes.

WICK SUPPORTS: Wooden cocktail sticks or skewers can be used to keep wicks vertical and centrally positioned in the mould while the molten wax is poured into it. The wick end is simply threaded onto or tied around the stick, which then rests across the shoulder of the mould, keeping the wick upright.

WICK SUSTAINERS: These are small metal discs with a hole in the centre, used to anchor the wick to the base of a mould that does not have a hole in it, such as a glass jar. Simply push the wick through the centre of the sustainer and pinch the metal to hold it securely in place.

waxes

Wax, of course, is the main ingredient used in candle making, and there are two main types used for most candle-making processes; paraffin wax and beeswax. Each has different qualities and is used in different ways or combinations to suit the project in hand. Paraffin wax, however, remains the most popular as it is relatively inexpensive, readily available and can be dyed any colour, shade or tint. There are also a number of specialist waxes available to be used as additives and for decorative effects.

APPLIQUÉ WAX: As the name suggests, this wax, which comes in very thin sheets that are easily cut into shapes with a craft knife, is used for achieving applied decorative effects. The beauty of it is that it can be pressed onto the surface of a candle without the use of glue. Appliqué wax is available in various different colours, as well as in a range of metallic finishes, and can also be bought ready-shaped into letters and numbers.

BEESWAX: A more expensive alternative to paraffin wax, beeswax is a natural product with a delicious, honey fragrance. It is available in block form or in sheets that have a honeycomb pattern imprinted onto the surface. Blocks are melted and moulded just like paraffin wax, whereas the sheets are used for making rolled candles. At room temperature beeswax sheets are soft, pliable and extremely easy to work with. In its natural form beeswax has a brownish colour, but it is also available bleached white and in a range of dyed colours.

COMMERCIAL PREPARED PARAFFIN WAX: Paraffin wax pellets can be obtained predyed with the correct amount of stearin and colour already added. They can be mixed together to form other colours or used with uncoloured wax to obtain lighter shades.

JELLY WAX: Jelly wax is a relatively new product and looks just like jelly, as the name suggests. It does not set hard like an ordinary wax, therefore, it cannot be cast in a mould but instead must be used in a container of some sort, preferably made of glass.

MICRO WAXES: These are added in varying proportions to paraffin wax to alter its setting time. Micro soft is added to allow the wax mixture to stay soft and malleable longer, which is useful for modelling projects. Micro hard is very hard and brittle when it is solid, and has a higher melting point than paraffin wax. It is used in the proportion of 1% with paraffin wax to strengthen candles and to make them slower burning.

MOULDABLE WAX: This soft wax is available in small, predyed quantities which can be moulded by hand, or using cookie cutters, to make small or floating candles. It is particularly easy for children to use.

PARAFFIN WAX: This is the basic ingredient required for most candle-making techniques. A by-product of the refining process of crude oil, paraffin wax is a translucent, odourless, tasteless substance. It is available in pellet form, which is very easy to use, or in slabs, which need to be broken up into smaller pieces before they can be used. At room temperature, paraffin wax is solid and it has a range of melting temperatures from 40–71°C (104–160°F). When it melts it is colourless and liquid, and when removed from the heat source it begins to solidify very quickly. In this semi-solid state, it is easy to cut, mould and embed objects into its surface to create various decorative effects.

STEARIN: This substance is often added to paraffin wax in a ratio of nine parts wax to one part stearin. It improves the burning quality and opacity of the candle and acts as a releasing agent when using rigid moulds.

WAX GLUE: This is wax, but in a very sticky form. A small amount is melted in a double boiler before sticking any form of decoration to the surface of a candle.

ready-made moulds

Ready-made candle moulds are now available in a huge variety of shapes and sizes. Rigid moulds are made from plastic, glass or metal, and are generally free-standing or, in the case of conical or pyramid shapes, are supplied with a small support. Flexible moulds are made from latex and need to be supported with card (see page 19).

CLEAR PLASTIC MOULDS: These are the moulds most commonly used in this book. Clear plastic moulds are strong and cheap, and as they are transparent they are useful when making multicoloured, layered or special effect candles. Spherical or egg-shaped candles can be made in two-part moulds. When using plastic moulds the wax should be heated to no more than 82°C (180°F).

FLEXIBLE MOULDS: These moulds are produced in a variety of shapes and sizes. Since they are made from a flexible material, latex, they can be produced in very intricate, irregular shapes with undercuts and deep reliefs. They do stretch and deteriorate in time, and are difficult to hold when they are full of hot wax. Use wax at a temperature of 93°C (200°F).

GLASS MOULDS: These produce high-gloss finished candles but are rather fragile and are limited to cylindrical shapes. Wax should be at a temperature of 82°C (180°F) when poured into glass moulds.

METAL MOULDS: Metal moulds are more expensive than their plastic counterparts but are longer-lasting, more durable and have an excellent cooling rate. Wax at up to 90°C (195°F) can be poured into them.

MOULD-MAKING KIT: You can also make your own flexible latex moulds using a special kit available from candle-making suppliers. This consists of a latex solution and a thickener that can be painted over a three-dimensional shape, such as a piece of fruit or a pebble, to make an individually shaped mould. Always follow the manufacturer's instructions when making flexible latex moulds. Wax is poured into these moulds at 93°C (200°F).

additions

Colours and scents can be added to your handmade candles to make them truly individual and personal. Some of the projects in this book also show you how to add three-dimensional objects to your candles, such as seashells, glass nuggets and mosaic tiles.

DYE DISCS: Wax dye discs are available in a range of basic colours and can be mixed to form a myriad of other shades. The amount needed to achieve the basic colour is recommended on the packet by the manufacturer, but for small quantities of wax it is more a matter of trial and error. Feel free to combine colours, or use as much or as little as you like to create the exact shade you want.

Dye disc colours are not as stable as dye powders, which means adjacent colours may bleed in time.

DYE POWDERS: These are very strong, and are usually used for commercial candle making. Only a very small amount is required to achieve an intense shade. These powders in particular are used to colour jelly wax.

SCENTS: Scents that can be used for candle making come in various forms and need to be oil-based so that they will dissolve in wax. Alcohol-based scents should not be used. Fragrance oils and scented wax beads are specially produced for candle making, and therefore do not affect the burning properties of the candle. To obtain correct quantities simply follow the manufacturer's instructions. Aromatherapy essential oils and dried or fresh herbs, flowers and spices are natural materials and may not always combine properly with the wax or burn well, so small quantities need to be tested first. The project on pages 72–74, Essential Scents, uses some tried and tested oils that work well with wax.

Once you have chosen your scent, simply add it to the molten wax before pouring it into a mould. The aroma is released when the candle burns.

making candles

The essential principles of candle making are much the same as they were in ages past. Of course modern technology has provided us with far superior materials and equipment, but the basic rules remain the same. Candles can be made with or without moulds, in a myriad of colours, shapes and textures. The following simple techniques form the basis upon which nearly all the projects in this book are designed. As candle making is a very creative craft (and sometimes for the beginner an unpredictable one) the projects serve not only to instruct, but also to inspire the new candle maker to add their own individuality, to create their own colours or to hand-make their own unique moulds, using many of the following techniques as a guide.

calculating quantities of paraffin wax and stearin

Remember that it is always better to heat too much wax rather than too little, since you can keep any leftover wax and remelt it for other projects. As you become used to working with wax you will be able to judge approximate quantities by eye, but to begin with, there is a basic general formula to follow when calculating the amount of wax you will need. Fill the mould you intend to use with water, then pour the water into a measuring jug. As a guide, 100 ml (5 fl oz) of liquid is approximately equivalent to 100 g (5 oz) in weight. For every 100 ml (5 fl oz) of water you will need to use 90 g (4½ oz) of paraffin wax and 10 g (½ oz) of stearin. You need to mix 90% paraffin wax and 10% stearin. If you are working with flexible moulds you do not need to add stearin, so should measure out 100% paraffin wax. If you are using commercial prepared wax you should also measure out 100% prepared wax.

When making multicoloured candles, the total amount must be divided into the various colours. When using jelly wax you need to judge by eye how much wax you will need to fill the mould, and then cut off the required amount accordingly.

heating the stearin

Place the required amount of stearin in a double boiler and melt it until it has turned into a clear liquid. You do not use stearin in flexible moulds.

adding dyes to the stearin or wax

A guide to using dye discs is given by the manufacturer, but generally, a whole disc will colour about 2 kg (4½ lb) of wax. To colour smaller quantities some trial and error is required. Dye discs can be cut into small pieces with a sharp knife, and then crushed with the back of a spoon. Always add a small amount at a time, then increase the amount if you want a darker shade. Test the colour with a strip of greaseproof paper. Simply dip the strip into the stearin, then, when it dries, you will be able to see the approximate finished shade.

If you are working with a flexible mould, and therefore not using stearin, simply add the dye to the wax alone, and test the colour in the same way.

adding the wax

Add the required amount of wax to the stearin and dye mixture, and heat in the double boiler until molten.

adding perfume

If you are making a scented candle this is the stage at which you add your scents. Simply add a few drops to the molten wax.

colouring jelly wax

Powder dyes are extremely strong, and are usually reserved for commercial usage, when large quantities of wax need to be dyed. However, if you are using jelly wax, this is the best type of dye to use. Only a very tiny amount is necessary to achieve a very strong colour. The colour you see in the boiler is pretty much the finished colour that will be achieved (1). Do take care not to spill any onto clothes or work surfaces, as it will stain badly and will be difficult to remove.

testing the temperature

Heat paraffin wax to the temperature specified in your project. Leave the thermometer in the wax and do not overheat the wax, as it could catch fire. As a general rule, wax used with rigid plastic, glass and cardboard moulds should be heated to 82°C (180°F). Wax used with flexible latex moulds should be heated to 93°C (200°F).

Heat jelly wax just until it is molten.

priming the wick

Cut the required length of wick for your project, then dip it into the molten wax in the double boiler (2). Lay it out flat on a piece of greaseproof paper. The wax will quickly

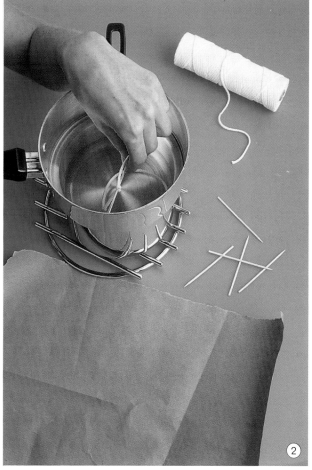

set and the wick will become hard and stiff. It is now ready to use. Priming ensures that a wick will have wax all through its length and will therefore burn properly. Priming can be done in advance, you may want to prime a whole length of wick to have it ready for use.

You should not prime the wick when working with a flexible latex mould, since the use of an unprimed wick decreases the risk of wax spillage.

positioning the wick

When using a rigid mould, cut the wick about 5 cm (2 in) longer than the height of the finished candle, prime it and pass it through the hole at the base of the mould. Secure the wick to a suitable wick support resting across the shoulder of the mould. Pull the wick taut at the base then secure and seal with a small blob of mould sealer.

When using a flexible mould, again, cut the wick about 5 cm (2 in) longer than the height of the finished candle, and thread a wicking needle with the unprimed wick. Gently push the needle through the base of the mould. Seal the wick with mould sealer and secure it to a suitable wick support resting across the shoulder of the mould.

multiwick

Candles that have a large diameter or width, or an unusual shape, often require more than one wick so that the wax will burn evenly. Suspend two or more lengths of primed wick across the top of your mould using suitable wick supports, making sure the wicks are evenly spaced apart (3).

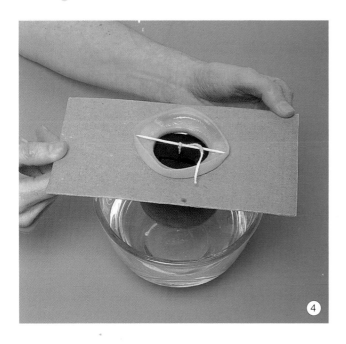

supporting a flexible mould

To secure a flexible mould over a water bath and while filling with wax, you will need some stiff card that is wider than the mouth of the water bath. Cut a hole in the centre of the card just large enough for the shoulder of the mould to fit in, and drop the mould into the support.

filling the mould

Whether you are using a flexible or rigid mould, fill it just over the shoulder with molten wax. Keep excess wax for topping up later. After a minute or two, gently tap the sides of the mould to release any trapped air bubbles. Now carefully lower the mould into the water bath, avoiding splashes. A flexible mould is supported by card around the shoulder of the mould and across the top of the bath (4). A rigid mould can have a weight placed on it. Allow the wax to cool.

topping up

After about one hour, pierce the wax around the wick with a cocktail stick. Then top it up with wax reheated to the previous temperature and allow to cool completely.

removing the candle from the mould

If you are using a rigid mould, when the candle is cold, remove the mould sealer and let the candle slide out. Trim the wick with a craft knife and then stand the candle in a warm, empty double boiler to level off the base. Trim the revealed wick to 1 cm (½ in), ready to light.

If you are using a flexible mould, when the wax is completely set, remove the mould from the water bath and rub a little liquid soap all over the surface. Remove the mould sealer and gently peel the mould away from the wax, releasing the candle (5). Trim away any excess wax from around the shoulder using a craft knife.

storing unused wax

Excess wax should be poured into a bowl lined with greaseproof paper. When it is completely cold it can simply be stored in a plastic bag and be reheated and used at a later stage.

making your own moulds

There are several methods you can use to make your own, individual candle moulds. Using a found container, such as a yoghurt pot or salad bowl, is a popular choice. Geometrical moulds can be formed from cardboard, while more intricate shapes can be made using a latex mould-making kit.

using found containers

Practically any watertight container can be used as a mould, tin cans, card tubes, yoghurt pots and milk or juice cartons, glass jars, salad bowls, even coconut shells, for example. The only consideration to be made is the shape.

The mould should either be straight sided or tapering towards the base. Using a mould that tapers towards the top is not entirely impractical but it does mean that the mould must be broken to release the candle.

Pierce a hole at the base of the mould and pass primed wick through, then seal the hole with mould sealer.

Alternatively, for more solid moulds, drop in a primed wick attached to a wick sustainer. Cast the candle using wax heated to 82°C (180°F). It may be necessary to cut a cardboard or plastic mould to release the candle when set.

making a flexible mould

A flexible rubber mould can easily be made using a non-porous object as a master. Place the object on a small upturned saucer or dish, then, following the manufacturer's instructions, apply several coats of latex mould-making solution using a paintbrush, allowing each coat to dry between applications. You will need to build up a coat about 3 mm (⅛ in) thick. For the last coat, mix the latex with the thickener provided in a ratio of 20:1. When the latex is dry, carefully peel it away from the master. Pierce a hole at the base of the mould and pass the unprimed wick through, then seal the hole with mould sealer. Cast the candle using wax, without stearin, heated to 93°C (200°F).

using open-ended containers

Open-ended card or plastic tubes, such as packaging materials or piping, can be used to make pillar candles. Place the tube onto a small piece of card and seal around the base with mould sealer. Pierce a hole in the base using a wicking needle and thread the primed wick through (1). Cast the candle as usual, using wax heated to 82°C (180°F). When the wax is cool, slice the tube open using a craft knife to release the candle.

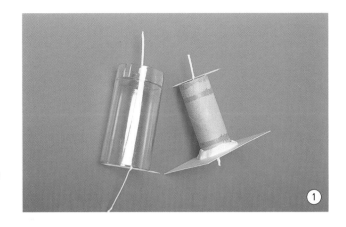

making your own card mould

Rigid moulds can be made using stiff or corrugated cardboard. Simply bend to the required shape using the templates provided, or design your own shape. Score and fold the card to construct the shape and fix overlaps in place using double-sided adhesive tape (2). Seal the joins with packing tape and wrap the entire mould with packing tape for added protection against leakage (3). Pierce a hole or holes in the base and thread the primed wick through, then seal with mould sealer (4). Cast the candle as usual, using wax heated to 82°C (180°F), and allow to cool. Then use a craft knife to slice open the mould to release the candle.

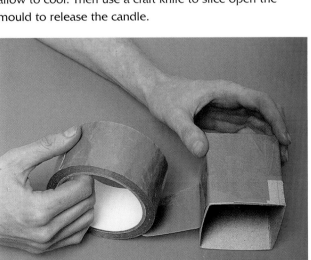

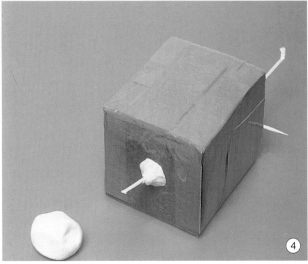

special effects

crackled candles

This delicate crackled effect can be applied over any set, smooth-sided candle. The finish is particularly effective when used over a strongly coloured candle.

Heat enough uncoloured paraffin wax to fill a dipping can to about 90% capacity – enough to cover the height of the finished candle without spilling over the edges of the can when you dip it in – to 88°C (190°F). Fill a bucket with cold water and add ice cubes to turn the water ice cold. Transfer the uncoloured paraffin wax to the dipping can. Hold the previously made candle firmly by the wick and dip the whole thing once into the molten wax. Immediately plunge the candle into the bucket of ice cold water. Upon removal you will see tiny crackles appearing all over the surface.

frosted candles

This popular effect is created very simply by pouring the wax into the mould at a very low temperature.

When the wax has melted, remove it from the heat and allow to cool, stirring continuously to prevent a skin forming on the surface. As the wax cools and you stir briskly you will see a little scum forming on the surface. Now pour a little wax into the prepared mould and swirl it around to coat the sides. Pour the wax back into the pan and stir again until frothy. Fill the mould with frothy wax and top up with wax cooled to 65°C (150°F).

embedded candles

Three-dimensional objects, such as shells and dried flowers, leaves and sliced fruit can be embedded into soft wax in the mould so that they can be viewed from the outside when the candle is released.

Cast the candle in the usual way. After about 10 minutes a thick skin, about 1 cm (½ in) thick, will have formed on top of the wax. Cut a hole in the skin with a sharp knife, and pour the still-molten wax in the centre

back into the double boiler. Working quickly, while the wax at the edges of the mould is still soft, press the pieces to be embedded firmly and deeply into the soft wax (1). Allow the wax to set. Remelt the wax in the double boiler and pour it back into the mould at no more than 73°C (165°F). Leave to set.

encrusted candles

You can cover the outside of your candle with decorative objects that are partly embedded.

First make an ordinary candle. Place this candle inside a second mould that is slightly wider than the first candle and resupport the wick as usual. Pour or spoon your chosen objects (such as grains or glass nuggets) between the sides of the two moulds. Remelt more paraffin wax to 82°C (180°F) and spoon it into the gap, to a height just above the first candle. Leave to set as usual.

embossed candles

An embossed effect can be achieved by gluing three-dimensional decorative plastic mouldings or thick card cutouts to the inside walls of a card mould before casting.

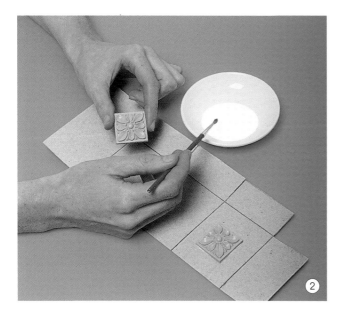

First cut out and score lines on the mould to be used. Use a household waterproof glue to fix the moulding or cutouts to one or all of the side walls, on the inside of the mould (2). Alternatively, card that is already embossed with a three-dimensional pattern can be used to make or line the mould. Make up the mould and cast as usual. When the wax is cold, slice open the mould using a craft knife to release the candle.

ice candles

This unusual effect is created by surrounding a ready-made candle in a slightly wider mould with crushed ice and molten wax.

Take a ready-made candle that is a little shorter and narrower than your mould. For this technique you need a candle no less than 2.5 cm (1 in) in diameter. Cut the candle to fit the mould if necessary. Place the candle in the mould and tie the wick to a suitable wick support. Do not seal the hole at the base of the mould. Fill the mould surrounding the candle with coarsely crushed ice and stand the mould in an empty bowl or on a plate that will catch the water as it melts. Pour in the prepared wax, heated to 99°C (210°F), and allow to cool (3).

pineapple candles

This interesting textured effect is very simply achieved by cooling a little wax in a bowl of cold water which turns it into brittle strands.

Prepare the mould and heat the wax as usual. Pour some of the wax in a steady stream into a bowl of cold water. The wax will solidify forming irregular strands on contact with the water. Take out the wax strands and pack them loosely into the mould. Let the remaining wax cool to about 65°C (150°F) and fill the mould as usual. Top up with wax cooled to the same temperature.

striped candles

Different coloured waxes may be used to make a striped or layered candle. It is best to use a clear plastic mould for this, so that you can see the levels, but if you want to use a specially designed card mould, simply make small marks on the outside with pen or masking tape, to guide you as you fill the mould.

Mix up your coloured wax and heat it to 82°C (180°F). Fill the mould to the height required. After a few minutes, gently tap the mould to release any air bubbles. Allow the first layer of wax to set until the surface feels rubbery to the touch. While you are waiting, heat another coloured wax to the same temperature. Pour the second layer onto the rubbery first stripe. Continue in the same way until you have built up the desired amount of layers. Top up the final layer and leave to cool as usual.

safety

Candle making is a relatively simple craft that can be done safely in your own kitchen at home, but it is important to follow a few necessary safety guidelines to avoid accidents and possible injury.

heating wax

Candle wax should be treated in the same way and with the same precautions as cooking oil, in that it should never be overheated or left unattended whilst being heated. Always heat wax in a double boiler as this ensures that the temperature does not exceed 100°C (212°F). Also, monitor the temperature regularly and carefully with a thermometer.

If the wax is heated to a temperature above 100°C (212°F) it begins to smoke and is then in real danger of ignition. In such an event, turn off the heat source immediately and then smother the flames with a damp tea towel or saucepan lid, do not try to extinguish the flame with water.

preparing the work area

Cover your work surfaces with sheets of newspaper, firstly to keep your kitchen worktop clean and secondly to catch drips and spills. When pouring hot wax into prepared moulds it can be helpful to place the mould in a baking tray or flat dish, just in case the mould leaks. Also this means that you can save the leaked wax for use later.

Keep moulds and equipment clean. Wash them in hot soapy water immediately after use, but remember never to pour wax down the sink as it will solidify in the U-bend and block up the plug hole.

Finally, try to keep all your equipment and materials to hand, it is essential that you do not leave the wax unattended while you look for that essential item.

treating spills

It is advisable, but not necessary, to wear an apron while candle making, just in case of spillage. Usually wax can be removed from clothing by ironing the garment between two sheets of brown paper that will absorb the wax. If wax falls onto the floor or a hard surface, just leave it to solidify then scrape it off using a spatula, or lift off small spots with your fingernail. A point to remember, however, is that some waxes are strongly coloured and may leave a stain behind.

using candles safely

After all your hard work it is now time to enjoy the fruits of your labour, there are, however, a few points to mention. Never leave a burning candle unattended, and remember to place candles in a safe position away from draughts or soft furnishings, curtains or any other flammable material. Always allow ample headroom above the candle flame for the heat to disperse – a point to remember if you have candles on shelves.

Be sure to choose the right candle holder. Use one that is steady and not likely to tip over and make sure that it is heat resistant. If using a holder with a spike, heat the spike with a match first, this will prevent the base of the candle from splitting when pushed in place.

Never burn a candle near another heat source or other electrical equipment.

Remember to keep candles well out of the reach of children and pets.

To extinguish a candle it is best to use a candle snuffer rather than just blowing out the flame. If the candle is large or in a container, there may be a well of molten wax formed around the wick. In this case, after the flame is extinguished, use a cocktail stick or a match stick to push the wick briefly into the wax so it is reprimed and ready for use next time.

Trim the candle wick before lighting and relighting, if the wick is longer than about 1 cm (½ in) the flame may smoke.

Always leave your newly made candles to rest for at least a day before lighting.

subtle slim

In this first section we learn the joy of candle making in the simplest of forms. The following projects have been grouped together because they all possess an element of simplicity and pureness, and as an introduction to candle making they require very little in the way of complicated technical knowledge.

We begin with Slim Jims, these smooth and simple elegant forms are cast from undyed wax in card moulds, then to fragrant hand-rolled beeswax pillars which require no mould or heating at all. Slender, fresh bamboo cane candles show how easy it is to make a flexible mould to produce an unusual, individual shape. The green apples also use a flexible mould, but this time a ready-made one, together with dye that is pre-prepared complete with apple scent. Jelly wax is a relatively new product that enables the candle maker to produce a stunning transparent candle contained in a simple glass vase, and a group of egg candles shows what can be created using ready-made two part moulds. With these projects under your belt, you will have mastered the basic techniques of candle making.

plicity

slim jims

The slender elegance of these oval candles is further enhanced by their simplicity and the minimalistic use of undyed wax. Make them in a range of different sizes and use them in a group for a display that will look beautiful even when unlit.

materials
tracing paper
stiff, shiny card
4 cm (1½ in) diameter wick and a wick sustainer
35 g (1½ oz) stearin
315 g (13½ oz) paraffin wax

additional equipment
pencil and scissors
ruler
double-sided adhesive tape
packing tape

PREPARING THE MOULD Photocopy the templates given on page 76 at 200%. Transfer the design to card and cut out. Score and fold along the dotted line using a ruler. Make sure the shiny surface of the card is facing inwards. Fold the rectangle around the oval base and fix in position using double-sided adhesive tape at the base of the rectangle. Seal the joins with packing tape. Put your hand inside the mould and open it up a little to form the slim oval shape. To make sure it is leakproof, wrap the entire mould with packing tape. Place the mould on a baking tray and fix it in place around the base using mould sealer. This will also prevent any wax leaking out.

PREPARING THE WICK Cut the wick about 5 cm (2 in) longer than the height of the finished candle and prime it (see page 17). Attach one end to a wick sustainer. Drop the wick into the mould and thread the free end through a cocktail stick or tie it to a wooden skewer. Rest the stick across the top of the mould so that it holds the wick vertically down the centre.

PREPARING THE WAX Melt the stearin in a double boiler. Add the paraffin wax and continue to heat until the wax is molten and reaches a temperature of 82°C (180°F).

FORMING THE CANDLE Pour the wax into the centre of the mould and set aside. Keep the excess wax for topping up later. After a few minutes, gently tap the sides of the mould to release any trapped air bubbles. Transfer the candle to a water bath and weigh it down. After about an hour a dip will form around the wick. Pierce the wax a few times with a cocktail stick then top up with wax reheated to 82°C (180°F). Leave to set completely.

FINISHING Remove the mould sealer and slice the mould open with a craft knife to release the candle. Remove the wick support and trim the revealed wick to about 1 cm (½ in).

To make the larger candle, photocopy the template to 350% and use 585 g (22½ oz) of paraffin wax with 65 g (2½ oz) of stearin.

tip

Candles made in cardboard moulds can have a cloudy or matt appearance. To achieve a soft sheen simply buff the surface of the candle firmly with a soft cloth.

naturally beeswax

Rolling sheets of preformed natural beeswax is probably the simplest and cleanest way of making candles. It takes almost no time at all and uses very little equipment to create beautiful and stylish candles. The triangular shape chosen for this project is an alternative to the usual round form, but is just as easy to make. Beeswax has a wonderful honey-like fragrance and, at room temperature, is soft, pliable and extremely easy to work with. No heating or gluing is required, the honeycombed texture and slightly tacky surface of each sheet enables the wax to stick to itself: only slight pressure from the hand is necessary to shape and hold the candle together.

materials
4 beeswax sheets
5 cm (2 in) diameter wick

additional equipment
metal ruler

PREPARING THE WICK Cut a length of wick about 2 cm (¾ in) longer than the height of the finished candle and prime it (see page 17). Press the wick firmly onto the short side edge of one beeswax sheet.

ROLLING Carefully curl the edge of the beeswax sheet tightly around the wick and then begin rolling up the whole sheet. When you reach the end, gently press the edge of the sheet into the rolled surface underneath.

SHAPING Take a metal ruler and lay the candle along its length. Press the ruler against the candle to make a flat side, then turn over and repeat, making another flat side at roughly a 60° angle to the first. Repeat once more, again at an approximately 60° angle, to create a softly rounded triangular shape. Press firmly along the length of all three sides with your fingers to make sure there are no gaps and the sides are fairly smooth.

BUILDING UP Lay another sheet of beeswax right up to the edge of the first sheet and press the two edges firmly together. Continue to roll up the sheet as before, following the triangular shape. Make sure that you roll evenly, so that all the edges remain at the same height. Reshape using the ruler as necessary.

FINISHING Add on another two sheets in the same way until the candle is complete. If you want to make a candle that is larger in diameter simply add on more sheets.

To make a more squat shape, use three sheets cut in half lengthways, thus creating six pieces in all.

tip

When making this type of candle, keep the beeswax warm, or it will tend to crack. Average room temperature is sufficient to keep the wax pliable, but if you do experience any problems, simply warm the sheets up a little using a hair dryer.

best bamboo

Making your own flexible mould is the only way to produce candles that are an unusual shape or have a delicate surface pattern. Latex mould-making materials are readily available and quite easy to use. For this project, use chunky lengths of bamboo as a master and you can make as many beautifully shaped candles as you like.

materials
20 cm (8 in) length of 4 cm (1½ in) diameter bamboo
4 cm (1½ in) diameter wick
stiff card
270 g (9½ oz) paraffin wax
¹⁄₁₀ of a green dye disc
liquid soap

additional equipment
sandpaper
small saucer
mould-making kit containing a latex mould-making
    solution and thickener
paintbrush
scissors

MAKING THE MOULD Sand the cut edges of the bamboo length to ensure that there are no rough edges. Fill the hollow ends using mould sealer to prevent the mould-making solution going down inside the bamboo. Stand the piece of bamboo on a small, upturned saucer and fix it in place with some more mould sealer. Following the manufacturer's instructions, apply several coats of the latex mould-making solution to the bamboo and saucer, you can either paint the solution on with a brush or spoon it over the master. Allow each coat to dry before applying the next. You will need to build up a layer about 3 mm (⅛ in) thick. For the last coat, mix the latex with the thickener in a ratio of 20:1, then stir well. When the mixture has thickened apply the final coat and then set aside. When completely dry, carefully peel the mould away from the master. Prepare a water bath, that will take the length of the candle.

PREPARING THE WICK AND MOULD Cut an unprimed wick about 5 cm (2 in) longer than the height of the finished candle and thread it through the eye of a wicking needle. Carefully pierce a hole at the base of the latex mould then draw the wick through. Seal the wick in place with mould sealer.

Fashion a support for the rubbery mould using stiff card that is wider than the neck of the water bath. Carefully cut a hole in the centre of the card, just large enough to fit around the shoulder of the mould. Place the mould into the card support, then pass a cocktail stick through the wick. Let the stick lie across the shoulder of the mould, holding it vertically in the centre of the mould.

PREPARING THE WAX Place the wax in a double boiler and heat to 93°C (200°F). Prepare the small amount of green dye disc to achieve the pale colouring, then crush roughly with the back of a spoon. Add the crushed dye to the molten wax and stir to dissolve. The greater the amount of dye used the stronger the colour will be, so start with a small amount and add more later if required. To get an idea of the approximate finished shade, dip a piece of greaseproof paper into the dyed wax and allow it to dry.

FORMING THE CANDLE Rest the card support over an empty container and carefully pour the wax into the mould, filling it to the shoulder. Keep the excess wax for topping up later. After a few minutes, gently tap the side of the mould to release any trapped air bubbles. Lower the filled mould into the water bath with the card supporting it, and set aside for about an hour. As the wax sets a dip will form around the wick. Pierce the wax a few times around the wick with a cocktail stick to prevent distortion. After another hour, top up with wax reheated to 93°C (200°F). Return the mould to the water bath until the wax is completely set.

FINISHING Remove the mould from the card support and cover the outside with liquid soap to facilitate easy removal. Carefully pull the rubber mould back on itself, releasing the bamboo shaped candle. Ease the wick from the base gently so as not to cause damage to the mould. Use a craft knife to trim any excess wax and wick from the base of the candle, levelling off any unevenness. Trim the revealed wick to about 1 cm (½ in).

green apples

Using commercial flexible moulds is an easy way of producing irregularly shaped candles or, in this case, very realistic fruit-shaped candles. However, there are a few things to remember when using flexible moulds. The wick must be unprimed since this decreases the risk of wax seepage. The mould will need to be supported by a rigid card template while the wax sets, ideally in a water bath, and stearin should not be used in the wax for this project as it will eventually rot the rubber.

materials
3 cm (1 ¼ in) diameter wick
stiff card
240 g (8½ oz) paraffin wax
approximately ¹/₇ of an apple-scented green dye disc
liquid soap

additional equipment
scissors
apple-shaped flexible latex mould
soft cloth

PREPARING THE WICK AND MOULD Cut the unprimed wick about 5 cm (2 in) longer than the mould and thread it through the eye of a wicking needle. Draw the needle and wick through the base of the mould, leaving a tail of 1.5 cm (⅝ in). This will eventually be the "stalk" of the finished apple candle. Seal it in place with mould sealer. Fashion a support for the flexible mould using stiff card that is wider than the mouth of the water bath. Carefully cut a hole in the centre of the card, just large enough to fit around the collar of the mould. Place the mould into the card support, then thread a cocktail stick through the wick and rest the stick across the shoulder of the mould, holding the wick vertically in the centre.

PREPARING THE WAX Place the wax in a double boiler and heat to 93°C (200°F). Crush the apple-scented green dye with the back of a spoon. This is enough for one fruit. Add the crushed dye to the molten wax and stir it in.

FORMING THE CANDLE Rest the card support over an empty container and pour the dyed wax into the mould, filling it to the shoulder. Keep the excess wax for topping up later. After a few minutes, gently tap the sides of the mould to release any trapped air bubbles. Transfer the mould to a water bath, with the card supporting it. After about an hour a dip will form around the wick. Use a cocktail stick to pierce the wax a few times around the wick. After another hour has elapsed, reheat the excess wax to 93°C (200°F) and use it to top up the mould. Set aside until the wax is completely set.

FINISHING Lift the mould from the support and remove the mould sealer and wick support. Cover the outside of the mould with liquid soap, then carefully pull the mould back on itself, easing the wick gently from the base so as not to damage the mould. Use a craft knife to trim any excess wax and wick from the base, levelling off any unevenness so the fruit will stand steadily by itself. Trim the revealed wick to about 1 cm (½ in). Finally, buff the wax to a subtle sheen using a soft cloth.

tip

Changing the water in the water bath about every 15 minutes during the first two hours will speed up the setting process.

jelly jar

Jelly wax is a relatively new product that can be used to create some really stunning visual effects. When the wax sets it looks and feels like jelly, and thus cannot be cast in a conventional mould, but instead should be supported in a decorative glass container.

materials
10 cm (4 in) diameter wick and a wick sustainer
1 kg (35 oz) jelly wax
pinch of violet powdered dye
glitter (optional)

additional equipment
glass container, 10 cm (4 in) diameter and
        18 cm (7 in) high
saucepan

PREPARING THE WICK Begin by cutting the wick about 5 cm (2 in) taller than the glass. Prime the wick as usual (see page 17). Thread one end of the wick into a wick sustainer. Place a tiny blob of mould sealer onto the underside of the wick sustainer then press it firmly to the base of the vase. Lay a wooden skewer across the top of the vase and tie the wick securely to it.

PREPARING THE WAX Place about 250 g (8¾ oz) of jelly wax into a double boiler over a low heat. The wax will begin to melt slowly. It is important here not to try to speed up the process by increasing the heat, as the wax will quickly become too hot and begin to smoke. Stir occasionally, and when all the wax is molten and fluid, add a tiny speck of violet powder dye at a time. This dye is intended for commercial use and is very concentrated. Fortunately, the colour does not change when the jelly sets so it is easy to judge the amount of dye to put in. When you are happy with the shade, remove the pan from the heat.

FORMING THE CANDLE Place a folded kitchen towel around the outside of the glass container to catch any drips. Pour the coloured jelly wax carefully into the vase and allow to set for about 15 minutes. While the wax is still molten in the vase you can sprinkle in some glitter for added effect. Repeat the process with another 250 g (8¾ oz) of the wax, but this time only put in about half the quantity of dye previously used. Pour, and allow to set as before. Then melt the remaining wax with no dye and pour it into the vase, only up to about 3 cm (1¼ in) from the top. Put the candle aside to set completely. Watch the colours merge, creating quite amazing colour changes.

FINISHING When the candle is cool, snip off the wick about 2 cm (¾ in) above the top of the wax: remember that neither the wick nor the flame should protrude above the top of the container.

tip

It is important to use powdered dye for this project to achieve good, transparent colours and not conventional dye discs, since technically the jelly is not "wax".

free-range eggs

Spherical or egg-shaped candles are easily formed by using ready-made, two-part moulds that are available in a variety of sizes. Here, the distinctive shape has been cast using three minimally different amounts of dye, to create pale, mid-tone and dark candles that look realistically egg-like. The following technique describes the amount of wax and stearin needed to make a single egg candle, but you may find it easier to make up more eggs using a higher weight of wax and stearin.

materials
2.5 cm (1 in) diameter wick

12 g (²⁄₅ oz) stearin (a 20% ratio of stearin to 80% paraffin wax is used to increase the opacity of the finished candle)

brown dye disc

48 g (1³⁄₅ oz) paraffin wax

additional equipment
clear plastic two-part egg mould, with a stand

PREPARING THE WICK Cut the wick about 5 cm (2 in) longer than the height of the finished candle and prime it (see page 17). Use a wicking needle to thread one end through the hole at the base of the bottom half of the mould (which will form the top part of the finished egg shape), then continue to thread it through the other half of the mould. Place the two halves of the mould together and seal around the join with mould sealer. At the base of the mould pull the wick taut, leaving about 1.5 cm (⁵⁄₈ in) revealed, and seal with mould sealer. Pass a cocktail stick through the other end of the wick and lay the stick across the top of the mould, holding the wick vertically down the centre.

PREPARING THE WAX Melt the stearin in a double boiler. Crush a sliver of brown dye with the back of a spoon and add it to the stearin, stirring to dissolve. To get an idea of the approximate finished shade, dip a strip of greaseproof paper into the dyed stearin and allow it to dry. Add more dye to achieve a darker, stronger colour.

Add the paraffin wax and heat until the wax is molten and reaches a temperature of 82°C (180°F).

FORMING THE CANDLE Pour the wax into the centre of the mould and keep the excess wax for topping up later. After a few minutes, gently tap the sides of the mould to release any trapped air bubbles. Transfer the mould to a water bath and weigh it down. Leave to set. After about an hour a dip will form around the wick. Pierce the wax a few times with a cocktail stick then top up with wax reheated to 82°C (180°F). Leave to set completely.

FINISHING Remove the mould sealer and the candle will slide easily out of the mould. Trim the wick at the base so the candle stands steadily, then trim the revealed end of the wick to about 1 cm (½ in).

To make darker eggs simply add more brown dye disc, but only do so a sliver at a time.

characte
cre

The following creations show how easy it is to achieve spectacular
effects based on texture, surface decoration and colour combinations,
just by using a few simple techniques. Most of the projects use
ready-made moulds, or very simple moulds made from card or latex.

Strange as it may seem the ubiquitous "frosted" look is, in fact, the
traditional candle-makers' nightmare. In purist terms the effect is
actually a "fault". These days however it is looked upon as very
attractive indeed and is simply achieved by pouring the wax at a very
low temperature, giving basic candle shapes a contemporary edge.

Temperature is the key factor in most of the special effects featured
in this section. Rapid cooling of freshly cast pyramid candles in a bath
of ice-cold water produces a delicately crackled effect on the surface.
The juicy Pineapple Pillars also employ the use of an ice-cold bath to

make molten wax into brittle strands that produce the "pineapple" effect. Last but not least, while we are on the subject of ice, is Ice Blue, cast in a plastic mould filled with crushed ice, which then melts causing the wax to set in the form of a labyrinth of delicate cavities.

Tapered Stripes and Rothko-esque feature the versatility of random striping of different coloured waxes. The tapered shape is cast in a large glass salad bowl mould, resulting in a characteristic smooth surface, while the Mark Rothko-inspired candle is made in a card mould which, in general, gives a soft, matt appearance.

A characteristic slant on surface decoration, citrus-coloured rectangular and square candles have pretty floral shapes embossed into the surface, while a group of stone-shaped candles is enhanced with simple hand-painting techniques.

frosted cubes

A group of four frosted candle cubes nestling neatly together would make a delightful centrepiece for a table or display area. The frosted effect is easily achieved and is extremely effective.

materials
6 cm (2⅜ in) diameter wick
270 g (9½ oz) green commercial prepared paraffin wax

additional equipment
clear plastic square-based pillar mould, 6 cm (2⅜ in) wide and 16 cm (6½ in) high
masking tape

PREPARING THE MOULD This technique involves moving the mould with the wax in it, so instead of filling a square mould to the top and therefore spilling the wax, you need to use a mould that is taller than the height of the finished candle. Simply mark the correct level by sticking a strip of masking tape to the outside of the mould at a height of 6 cm (2⅜ in) from the base.

PREPARING THE WICK Cut the wick about 5 cm (2 in) longer than the height of the finished candle and prime it (see page 17). Use a wicking needle to thread the wick through the hole at the base of the mould. Tie the end of the wick to a wooden skewer. Rest the stick across the top of the mould, holding the wick vertically down the centre. At the base of the mould pull the wick taut and then seal with mould sealer.

tips

Remember that the frosting effect causes the wax to appear much lighter in colour and take this into consideration when choosing your coloured wax.
   If a group of finished candles differ in height, just stand each in a warm, empty double boiler to melt and level off the base so they will match each other exactly.

PREPARING THE WAX Heat the green commercial prepared paraffin wax in a double boiler until molten.

THE FROSTING TECHNIQUE Remove the wax from the heat and allow to cool, stirring continuously to prevent a skin forming. Soon you will see a little scum developing on the surface. When this happens, pour a little wax into the mould. Swirl the wax around the mould to coat the inside, just up to the marked level, then pour the wax back into the pan. Stir the wax again, quite briskly, until it becomes frothy. Refill the mould up to the mark and keep the excess wax for topping up later. After a few minutes, tap the sides of the mould to release any trapped air bubbles that could ruin the finished effect. Transfer the mould to a water bath and weigh it down. After about an hour a dip will form around the wick. Pierce the wax a few times around the wick with a cocktail stick, then top up to the marked level with molten wax cooled to a temperature of no more than 65°C (150°F). Leave to set completely.

FINISHING The cold candle will slide easily out of the mould when the mould sealer is removed. Trim the wick at the base so that the candle stands steadily, then remove the wick support and snip the revealed wick to about 1 cm (½ in).
   Make another green frosted candle and two blue ones in exactly the same way, to complete the set.

tapered stripes

These chunky tapering shapes were inspired by simple glass salad bowls, that can be found in many sizes and were actually used here as moulds. The stripy candle was built by layering red and undyed wax, which takes on the colour of the surrounding red layers to create an individual pink shade. Any container can be used in the same way, provided it is fairly rigid and watertight. A candle this size needs more than one wick to ensure that the wax burns evenly.

materials

13 mm (½ in) diameter wick and 3 wick sustainers
200 g (7 oz) stearin
2 red dye discs
1.8 kg (4 lb) paraffin wax (for the red layers)
60 g (2 oz) stearin
540 g (19 oz) paraffin wax (for the middle layer)

additional equipment

tapered glass salad bowl, approximately 8 cm (3¼ in)
    base diameter, 20 cm (8 in) top diameter and
    12 cm (4¾ in) high
masking tape

PREPARING THE WICK Cut three wicks about 5 cm (2 in) longer than the height of the finished candle and prime them (see page 17). Attach one end of each primed wick to a wick sustainer. Drop the wicks into the mould, evenly spaced apart, and tie the free ends to two or three wooden skewers. Lay the sticks across the top of the salad bowl mould so that they hold the wicks vertically inside the mould.

PREPARING THE WAX Melt the first quantity of stearin in a double boiler. Crush both red dye discs with the back of a spoon. Add the crushed dye to the melted stearin and stir to dissolve. To test the colour, dip a strip of greaseproof paper into the dyed stearin. When it dries you will be able to see an approximate finished shade. Add more dye to make a deeper, darker colour.

Add the first quantity of paraffin wax to the dyed stearin and continue to heat until the wax is molten and reaches a temperature of 82°C (180°F).

FORMING THE CANDLE Mark the outside of the salad bowl with masking tape strips indicating the height of each stripe you want to make. The first mark here is approximately 5 cm (2 in) up from the base of the bowl and the second is approximately 3 cm (1¼ in) above that. Pour the red wax into the centre of the mould and fill to the first mark. Retain the excess for the final layer. Set the mould aside for a few minutes, then gently tap the sides to release any trapped air bubbles. Allow the wax to set until it is quite rubbery to the touch.

While the first layer is setting, mix up a batch of undyed wax, using the second quantity of stearin and paraffin wax. As soon as the first layer has set to a

rubbery consistency, pour on the middle layer of undyed wax, up to the second mark on the mould. Allow to set as for the first layer. To get the red wax to blend in with the undyed wax it is essential that you do not let each layer of wax set too solid. Finally, add another layer of red wax to almost fill the mould. Keep excess wax for

topping up later. After about an hour a dip will form around the wicks. Pierce the wax a few times with a cocktail stick then top up with wax reheated to 82°C (180°F). Leave to set completely.

FINISHING When the wax is cold the candle will slide easily out of the mould. Remove the wick supports and trim the wicks down to 1 cm (½ in).

To make the solid coloured tapered candles, use a salad bowl approximately 10 cm (4 in) base diameter, 25 cm (10 in) top diameter and 15 cm (6 in) high. Use 300 g (10 oz) of stearin and 2.7 kg (6 lb 6 oz) of paraffin wax and six red dye discs for the claret candle, or two red dye discs for the paler candle.

tip

Y ou can, of course, make several candles in different sizes and with varying colour combinations. Cream looks good interspersed between colours, and candles formed using different shades of just one colour are also very attractive.

crackled pyramids

All that is required to produce this dramatic effect is a bucket of ice-cold water. Dip a set candle once in uncoloured paraffin wax, then plunge it immediately into the water. The sudden change in temperature causes the outer layer of uncoloured wax to craze, producing a delicate pattern of tiny crackles all over the surface, almost ceramic in appearance. The effect is more pronounced on a strongly coloured candle, so for this project a deep rich amber is mixed using two commercial precoloured waxes.

materials
5 cm (2 in) diameter wick
200 g (7 oz) yellow commercial prepared paraffin wax
90 g (3 oz) red commercial prepared paraffin wax
ice cubes
900 g (32 oz) uncoloured paraffin wax

additional equipment
clear plastic pyramid mould, 6 cm (2⅜ in) wide
    and 23 cm (9 in) high
1 kg (35 oz) capacity dipping can
large bowl, such as a dishwashing bowl
tea cloth

PREPARING THE WICK Cut the wick to about 5 cm (2 in) longer than the height of the finished candle and prime it (see page 17). Use a wicking needle to draw the wick through the hole at the base of the mould. Pull the wick taut at the base, leaving about 1.5 cm (⅝ in) revealed, and seal with mould sealer. Tie the other end of the wick around a wooden skewer and rest the stick across the shoulder of the mould, holding the wick vertically down the centre of the mould.

PREPARING THE WAX Put both the yellow and red commercial prepared coloured waxes into a double boiler and heat until the wax is molten and reaches a temperature of 82°C (180°F).

FORMING THE CANDLE Pour the wax into the mould and set aside. Keep the excess wax for topping up later. After a few minutes, gently tap the sides of the mould to release any trapped air bubbles. Transfer the mould to a water bath and weigh it down. After about an hour a dip will form around the wick. Pierce the wax a few times with a cocktail stick. After another hour has elapsed, reheat the wax left in the boiler to 82°C (180°F) and use it to top up the mould. Leave to set completely. Remove the mould sealer and slide the candle out of the mould. Do not trim the wick yet.

THE CRACKLING TECHNIQUE Add ice cubes to a bucket of cold water. Leave to stand for a few minutes until all the water is ice cold. Heat the uncoloured paraffin wax in a clean double boiler to a temperature of 88°C (190°F). Carefully transfer the wax to a dipping can. Hold the set pyramid candle firmly by the wick and dip it once into the molten wax, taking care to cover the entire candle from tip to base. Then immediately plunge the candle into the bucket of ice-cold water. Keep the candle submerged for a few minutes until the dipped layer is completely cold and set. Remove the candle and watch the cracks as they form. Dry the candle with a tea cloth and trim the wick at the base so the candle stands steadily. Trim the revealed wick to about 1 cm (½ in).

tip

This effect can also be achieved by placing a warm, half-set candle into the icebox of the refrigerator. The wax will cool very rapidly, resulting in a similar crackled surface appearance; however, the crackles will be much larger.

pineapple pillars

These juicy, citrus coloured pillar candles look almost like crushed pineapple. The effect is created simply by pouring some hot wax into a bowl of cold water, then filling the mould with the resulting brittle strands. The rest of the mould is then refilled with molten wax as usual.

materials
7.5 cm (3 in) diameter wick
100 g (3½ oz) stearin
¼ of a yellow dye disc
900 g (31½ oz) paraffin wax

additional equipment
mould: any large, tubular, watertight
    food container, such as that used
    for stacking crisps and dried fruit,
    approximately 7 cm (2¾ in) diameter
    and 20 cm (8 in) high
scissors
bradawl
large bowl, such as a dishwashing bowl
fork

PREPARING THE MOULD Cut the mould to size if necessary. Using a bradawl, pierce a hole in the centre of the base of the mould. Fill a large bowl with cold water for use later.

PREPARING THE WICK Cut the wick about 5 cm (2 in) longer than the height of the finished candle and prime it (see page 17). Use a wicking needle to thread one end of the wick through the hole at the base of the mould. Pass a cocktail stick through the wick and rest the stick across the top of the mould, holding the wick vertically down the centre of the mould. At the base of the mould pull the wick taut and seal with mould sealer.

PREPARING THE WAX Melt the stearin in a double boiler. Crush the yellow dye with the back of a spoon and add it to the stearin, stirring to dissolve. To get an idea of the approximate finished shade, dip a strip of greaseproof paper into the dyed stearin and allow it to dry. Add more dye to achieve a darker, stronger colour.

Add the paraffin wax and heat until the wax is molten and reaches a temperature of 82°C (180°F).

THE TEXTURING TECHNIQUE Pour approximately half of the wax in a steady stream into the bowl of cold water. The wax cools rapidly on contact with the water, forming irregular brittle strands. Use a fork to scoop the strands out of the water, shake off the excess drips, then loosely pack them into the mould. Reheat the remaining wax until molten and then let it cool to about 65°C (150°F). Pour it into the centre of the mould, filling it to the top. The refill temperature must be lower than usual, otherwise the delicate strands will melt and the effect would be ruined. Keep the excess wax for topping up later. After a few minutes, gently tap the sides of the mould to release any trapped air bubbles. After about an hour a dip will form around the wick. Pierce the wax a few times with a cocktail stick then top up with wax cooled to 65°C (150°F). Leave to set completely.

FINISHING When cold the candle should slide from the mould easily when the mould sealer is removed. If you experience any difficulty, simply slice the mould open with a craft knife to release the candle. Trim the wick at the base so that the candle stands steadily, then remove the wick support and trim the revealed wick to 1 cm (½ in).

To make the squat orange pineapple pillar use the same amount of wax and stearin and ⅓ of an orange dye disc in a "found" or plastic mould 10 cm (4 in) in diameter and 12 cm (4¾ in) high. For the mid-sized orange textured candle use 540 g (19 oz) of paraffin wax and 60 g (2 oz) of stearin with ¼ of an orange dye disc in a plastic or "found" mould 7.5 cm (3 in) in diameter and 16 cm (6½ in) high.

rothko-esque

The subtle, muted colours of Mark Rothko paintings were the inspiration for this rectangular, double wick candle. As a card mould is constructed for its casting it is difficult to see how the layers are forming, however, it is exciting to open up the mould and see the finished result.

materials
tracing paper
stiff, shiny card
5 cm (2 in) diameter wick
200 g (7 oz) dark blue commercial prepared paraffin wax
200 g (7 oz) blue commercial prepared paraffin wax
200 g (7 oz) orange commercial prepared paraffin wax
200 g (7 oz) red commercial prepared paraffin wax

additional equipment
pencil and scissors
ruler
double-sided adhesive tape
packing tape

PREPARING THE MOULD Photocopy the template on page 77 to 400%. Trace and transfer it to stiff card and cut out. Score along the dotted lines and bend the card, using a ruler, to form a rectangular box with the shiny surface facing inwards. Use a pencil to clearly mark the height of each layer you want to build up on the inside of the mould before taping it together. Fix the side overlap into position using double-sided adhesive tape. Fold the flaps under at the base and fix with double-sided tape. Wrap the entire mould with packing tape to seal all the joins and prevent possible seepage.

PREPARING THE WICKS Cut two wicks about 5 cm (2 in) longer than the height of the finished candle and prime them (see page 17). Use a wicking needle to pierce two evenly spaced holes through the base of the mould, then thread one end of each wick through each hole. Tie the wick ends to a wooden skewer and lay it across the top of the mould holding the wicks vertically. At the base of the mould pull the wicks taut and seal with mould sealer.

Place the mould on a baking tray sealed around the base with more mould sealer, to fix it in place.

PREPARING THE WAX Melt the dark blue wax in a double boiler until it is molten and reaches a temperature of 82°C (180°F).

FORMING THE CANDLE Pour the dark blue wax into the centre of the mould, up to the first pencil mark. After a few minutes, gently tap the sides of the mould to release any trapped air bubbles.

BUILDING UP LAYERS Prepare the blue wax in the same way as before. Allow the first layer of wax to become rubbery to the touch, then pour in the second layer, and, after a few minutes, gently tap the mould to release any trapped air bubbles. Continue working in the same way with the orange and red waxes. Keep some excess red wax for topping up later. Set the candle aside. After about an hour a dip will form around each wick. Pierce the surface of the wax a few times with a cocktail stick then top up with wax reheated to 82°C (180°F). Leave to set.

FINISHING When the wax is completely cold, remove the mould sealer and wick supports and slice open the mould with a craft knife. Snip off the wicks level with the base and trim the revealed wicks to 1 cm (½ in).

troubleshooting

If the stripes are undefined in the finished candle it means that the layers were not set enough to support each other. Make sure the surface of the previous layer is rubbery to the touch before pouring on the next.

ice blue

Ice candles are made, as the name suggests, with the help of ice. The molten wax is poured over crushed ice contained in a wide pillar mould that has a 2.5 cm (1 in) diameter bought candle as a core. The wax cools quickly creating a fascinating labyrinth of irregular cavities. When the ice melts the water can be poured away. The core candle protects the wick from moisture ensuring that the candle lights and burns as normal.

materials

blue ready-made candle, 2.5 cm (1 in) diameter and 13 cm (5½ in) high
ice cubes (enough to fill the space between the ready-made candle and the edges of the mould)
approximately 270 g (9½ oz) blue commercial prepared paraffin wax

additional equipment

clear plastic pillar mould, 8 cm (3¼ in) diameter and 13 cm (5½ in) high
glass bowl
tea cloth
rolling pin

PREPARING THE READY-MADE CANDLE Place the ready-made candle in the centre of the mould. Do not seal the hole in the mould, since this is needed for drainage as the ice melts. Tie the wick of the bought candle to a wooden skewer and rest the skewer across the shoulder of the mould.

tips

Use a clear plastic mould for these candles since it is exciting to see the pattern that the wax and ice form and to watch the whole process.
Try to ensure that the core candle remains vertical in the centre of the mould.

PREPARING THE ICE Stand the mould in a glass bowl that will catch the water as the ice melts. Wrap some ice cubes in a clean tea cloth and strike them with a rolling pin to crush them. The size of the pieces of crushed ice will determine the appearance of the finished candle, larger pieces will create larger cavities, finer pieces will create smaller, more delicate cavities. Fill the mould to the top with coarsely crushed ice.

PREPARING THE WAX Place the blue commercial prepared wax in a double boiler and heat until the wax is molten and reaches a temperature of 99°C (210°F).

FORMING THE CANDLE Pour the wax carefully down one side of the mould containing the ice and the ready-made candle. Continue pouring until the mould is full. The amount of wax you need will depend on the amount of ice in the mould, so do not be surprised if you have some left over. Simply transfer the excess to a bowl lined with greaseproof paper and allow to set. The solid wax can then be remelted and used again at a later date.

Set the candle aside for about an hour. As the ice melts the water will pour away through the hole in the mould and into the bowl below.

FINISHING Remove the wick support and slide the candle from the mould. There may be a few pieces of ice that remain inside, but they will soon melt and the water will run off. Allow the candle to stand until completely dry. Trim the revealed wick to about 1 cm (½ in).

floral embossed

Inexpensive plastic decorative mouldings are used here to create pretty embossed flower patterns in the surface of these citrus coloured rectangular and square candles.

materials
tracing paper
stiff shiny card
waterproof glue
5 cm (2 in) diameter wick
300 g (10½ oz) orange commercial prepared paraffin wax

additional equipment
pencil and scissors
decorative plastic moulding, 10 cm (4 in) wide and
      6 cm (2⅜ in) high
ruler
double-sided adhesive tape
packing tape

PREPARING THE MOULD Photocopy the rectangular template given on page 77 at 200%, then trace and transfer it to stiff card. Cut out the design and score and fold along the dotted lines using a ruler, with the shiny surface facing inwards. Glue the decorative plastic moulding to one long, shiny, side of the mould. Bend the card into shape, then fix the side overlap securely with double-sided adhesive tape. Bend the base flaps under and fix with double-sided adhesive tape. Wrap the entire mould with packing tape to seal all joins.

PREPARING THE WICK Cut two wicks about 5 cm (2 in) longer than the height of the finished candle and prime them (see page 17). Use a wicking needle to pierce two holes through the base of the mould, then thread the wicks through the holes. Tie the wick ends to a wooden skewer and lay the stick across the top of the mould, holding the wicks vertically in the mould. At the base of the mould pull the wicks taut and seal with mould sealer.

Place the mould on a baking tray and seal around the base with more mould sealer, to fix it in place and prevent wax leaking out.

PREPARING THE WAX Melt the orange commercial prepared paraffin wax in a double boiler until the wax is molten and reaches a temperature of 82°C (180°F). Pour the wax into the centre of the mould filling it to the top, then set aside. Keep excess wax for topping up later. After a few minutes, gently tap the sides of the mould to release any trapped air bubbles. After about an hour a dip will form around the wicks. Pierce the wax a few times with a cocktail stick then top up with wax reheated to 82°C (180°F). Leave to set completely.

FINISHING When the wax is cold, remove the mould sealer and slice open the mould with a craft knife to release the candle. Prize the card carefully from the sides so as not to damage the embossed pattern. Remove the wick support and snip off the wicks at the base. Trim the other ends to about 1 cm (½ in). To make the yellow embossed cube candle, use the cube template on page 77 at 200% and stick a 3 cm (1¼ in) square decorative moulding with a flower pattern onto the inside of the card mould. Use 270 g (9½ oz) of yellow commercial prepared wax and a single wick.

zenstones

Realistic stone-shaped candles in subtle shades of grey look enchanting when grouped together, perhaps as a centrepiece for a dinner table or as part of a small indoor water feature. A candle mould based around a real pebble can be made using a latex mould-making kit.

materials

1 palm-sized pebble
5 cm (2 in) diameter wick
stiff card
800 g (28 oz) paraffin wax
black dye disc
chalky white dye disc
black pigment
liquid soap
white acrylic paint

additional equipment

small saucer
mould-making kit containing a latex mould-making
    solution and thickener
paintbrush
scissors
stencil brush
soft cloth

MAKING THE MOULD Clean and dry the pebble and place it on an upturned saucer. Following the manufacturer's instructions, apply several coats of the latex mould-making solution to the pebble and saucer, allowing each coat to dry a little before applying the next. Aim to build up a layer that is about 3 mm (⅛ in) thick. For the final coat, mix the latex solution with the thickener in a ratio of 20:1, then stir well. When the mixture has thickened, apply the final coat then set aside. When completely dry, carefully peel the mould away from the master.

PREPARING THE WICK AND MOULD Cut an unprimed wick about 5 cm (2 in) longer than the height of the finished candle and thread it through the eye of a wicking needle. Carefully pierce a hole at the base of the mould

with the needle then draw the wick through. Pull the wick taut at the base, leaving about 1.5 cm (⅝ in) revealed, and seal in place with mould sealer.

Make a support for the rubbery mould using stiff card that is wider than the neck of the water bath. Carefully cut a hole in the centre of the card, just large enough to fit around the shoulder of the mould. Place the mould into the card support, then pass a cocktail stick through the wick. Let the stick lie across the shoulder of the mould, holding the wick vertically in the centre of the mould.

PREPARING THE WAX Place the paraffin wax in a double boiler and heat to 93°C (200°F). To make a black pebble candle add a tiny amount of black pigment to the wax. To make a lighter, grey pebble candle use small portions of black dye disc and add a little chalky white. Cut a small piece off the disc then crush roughly with the back of a spoon. Add the crushed dye to the molten wax and stir to dissolve. The greater the amount of dye used the stronger the colour will be, so start with a small amount and add more later if required. To get an idea of the approximate finished shade, dip a strip of greaseproof paper into the dyed wax and allow it to dry.

FORMING THE CANDLE Rest the card support over an empty container and carefully pour the dyed wax into the mould, filling it to the shoulder. Keep excess wax for topping up later. After a few minutes, gently tap the mould to release any trapped air bubbles. Lower the filled mould into a water bath with the card supporting it, and set aside for an hour. As the wax sets a dip will form around the wick. Pierce the wax a few times wick with a cocktail stick. After another hour, top up with wax reheated to 93°C (200°F). Return the mould to the water bath until the wax is completely set.

FINISHING Remove the mould from the card support and cover the outside with liquid soap to facilitate easy removal. Carefully pull the rubber mould back on itself, releasing the pebble candle. Ease the wick from the base gently so as not to damage the mould. Use a craft knife to trim any excess wax and wick from around the base of the candle, levelling off any unevenness so that the candle will stand steadily by itself. Trim the revealed wick to about 1 cm (½ in).

To create a mottled effect, simply stipple a little white acrylic paint onto the candle using a stencil brush.

To make other stone candles, use different sizes or shapes of pebbles as masters for the mould and vary the colours of the wax for a natural look.

frosted pillars

The very popular frosted, scaly appearance of these sturdy pillars is simply created by pouring the wax into the mould at a very low temperature. The wax is stirred while cooling, to create a frothy texture. For a fluffier, lighter look, you could use a wire whisk to whip up the cool wax.

materials
5 cm (2 in) diameter wick
60 g (2 oz) stearin
¼ of a blue dye disc
540 g (19 oz) paraffin wax

additional equipment
clear plastic pillar mould, 6 cm (2⅜ in) diameter and
    20 cm (8 in) high
masking tape

PREPARING THE MOULD This technique involves moving the mould with the wax in it, so you need to use a mould that is taller than the height of the finished candle. Mark the mould with a strip of masking tape, 18 cm (7 in) from the base to make the tallest candle.

PREPARING THE WICK Cut the wick about 5 cm (2 in) longer than the height of the finished candle and prime it (see page 17). Use a wicking needle to thread one end through the hole at the base of the mould. Tie the free end around a wooden skewer and lay the skewer across the top of the mould holding the wick vertically down the centre. At the base of the mould pull the wick taut and seal with mould sealer.

PREPARING THE WAX Melt the stearin in a double boiler. Crush the blue dye with the back of a spoon. Add the dye to the stearin and stir to dissolve. The greater the amount of dye used the stronger the colour will be, so start with a small amount and add more later if required. To get an idea of the approximate finished shade, dip a strip of greaseproof paper into the dyed wax and allow it to dry.

Add the paraffin wax and heat until the wax is molten and reaches a temperature of 82°C (180°F).

THE FROSTING TECHNIQUE Remove the wax from the heat and allow to cool, stirring continuously to prevent a skin forming on the surface. Soon you will see a little scum developing on the surface. When this happens, pour a little wax into the mould. Swirl the wax around the mould to coat the inside up to the mark, then pour the wax back into the pan. Stir the wax again quite briskly until it becomes frothy. Refill the mould up to the mark and keep excess wax for topping up later. After a few minutes, gently tap the sides of the mould to release any trapped air bubbles. Transfer the candle to a water bath and weigh it down. After about an hour a dip will form around the wick. Pierce the wax a few times with a cocktail stick then top up to the marked level with wax heated and then cooled down to a temperature of about 65°C (150°F). Leave to set completely.

FINISHING The cold candle will slide easily out of the mould when the sealer is removed. Remove the wick support and snip off the wick level with the base. Trim the revealed end of the wick to about 1 cm (½ in).

Make another frosted pillar in the same way using violet dye. To make the shorter pillars, mark the mould with masking tape 15 cm (6 in) from the base and use 450 g (16 oz) of paraffin wax with 50 g (2 oz) of stearin and just under ¼ of a dye disc.

> **tip**
>
> The frosting technique causes the finished candle to appear much lighter in colour, so remember to take this into consideration when adding your dye disc to the stearin.

additional
embell

Having mastered the basic techniques of candle making, plus a few clever tricks of the trade, try some more adventurous projects that feature the embellishment of simple wax shapes, using a host of decorative objects from anywhere around the home, garden or from craft shops. You could even use the information in the following section as a starting point for the creation of themed displays for your home.

Embedding is an important method of embellishment, together with simple appliqué techniques. Essentially, embedding is the insertion of objects such as shells, glass nuggets, grains or anything else you can think of, into the outer layer of wax that surrounds the candle. Lustred Light and the Grain-covered Pillars use a technique featuring two moulds, while the Seashell Square is formed from "walls" of wax that allow the shells to protrude from the surface.

Wafer-thin, flexible, self-adhesive appliqué wax is available in a vast array of colours, metallic finishes and holographic effects. Our wire effect Metallic Ideas shows just a few ways to use this infinitely versatile product. Alternatively, wax glue is a wonderful invention and can be used to firmly attach small decorative objects, such as mirror mosaic tiles, to the surface of a finished candle.

Finally, the recent popularity of aromatherapy prompted the inclusion of a delightful little collection of fragrant container candles. Deliciously scented sorbet-coloured candles are cast in frosted glass vessels and have both decorative and therapeutic uses.

shments

lustred light

Colourful glass nuggets are often seen at the base of a water bowl containing floating candles. Here, however, the nuggets are actually embedded within the candle, giving a shimmering lustre to a simple square shape.

materials
5 cm (2 in) diameter wick
50 g (2 oz) stearin
450 g (16 oz) paraffin wax
selection of colourful glass nuggets

additional equipment
clear plastic square mould 6 cm (2⅜ in) wide and
    7.5 cm (3 in) high
clear plastic square mould, 8 cm (3¼ in) wide and
    10 cm (4 in) high

PREPARING THE WICK Cut the wick about 5 cm (2 in) longer than the height of the finished candle and prime it (see page 17). Use a wicking needle to thread one end through the hole at the base of the first mould. Tie the free end around a wooden skewer and lay the skewer across the top of the mould holding the wick vertically

down the centre. At the base of the mould pull the wick taut and seal with mould sealer.

PREPARING THE WAX Melt the stearin in a double boiler, then add the paraffin wax. Continue heating the wax until it is molten and reaches a temperature of 82°C (180°F).

FORMING THE CANDLE Pour as much of the wax as will fit into the centre of the mould, filling it to the top. Keep the excess wax for topping up and embedding the nuggets later. After a few minutes, gently tap the mould to release any trapped air bubbles. After about an hour a dip will form around the wick. Pierce the wax a few times with a cocktail stick then top up with wax reheated to 82°C (180°F). Leave to set completely.

ADDING THE NUGGETS When the candle is cold, remove the mould sealer and wick support and slide the candle out of the mould. Do not trim the wick yet.

Place the square candle inside the second clear plastic mould. Thread the wick through the hole in the mould and seal it with mould sealer, then attach a wick support to the other end. Position the nuggets between the sides of the two moulds to fill the gap. Remelt the remaining paraffin wax in the double boiler. When the mixture has reached 82°C (180°F), pour or spoon it into the gap between the moulds covering the nuggets to a height just above the first candle. Leave to set.

FINISHING When cold, remove the mould sealer and wick support and slide the candle out of the mould. Trim the wick at the base so that the candle stands steadily and snip the revealed end to about 1 cm (½ in).

Use the same technique to make any number of candles using different coloured nuggets.

mirror mosaic

In this project, glass mirror tiles are glued around the surface of the candle using specialist wax glue. This technique can be carried out using a multitude of decorative materials, such as dried flowers and leaves or colourful buttons for a great range of finished effects. The small, reflective, mirror mosaic tiles used here not only create a dazzling display when the candle is used alone, but will also reflect the warm flickering light from other candles when positioned within a group.

materials
10 cm (4 in) diameter wick and 3 wick sustainers
100 g (3½ oz) stearin
⅕ of a red dye disk
900 g (31½ oz) paraffin wax
selection of mirror mosaic tiles
wax glue

additional equipment
plastic piping (from a builder's merchant) approximately
    10 cm (4 in) diameter and 14 cm (5½ in) high
tile nippers (optional)

PREPARING THE MOULD Place the plastic piping on some greaseproof paper on a baking tray and seal all around the base with mould sealer.

PREPARING THE WICK Cut three wicks about 5 cm (2 in) longer than the height of the finished candle and prime (see page 17). Attach one end of each to a wick sustainer.

PREPARING THE WAX Melt the stearin in a double boiler. Crush the red dye with the back of a spoon and add it to the melted stearin, stirring to dissolve. Dip a strip of greaseproof paper into the dyed stearin. When it dries you will be able to see an approximate finished shade. Add more dye to make a deeper, darker colour.

Add the paraffin wax to the dyed stearin and continue to heat until the wax is molten and reaches a temperature of 82°C (180°F). Pour a thin layer of wax into the centre of the mould. After a few minutes, drop the prepared wicks into the molten wax, evenly spaced apart. Tie the free ends around two wooden skewers and lay the sticks across the top of the mould, holding the wicks vertically.

FORMING THE CANDLE Reheat the wax to a temperature of 82°C (180°F) and pour it into the centre of the mould to fill it. Keep the excess wax for topping up later. After a few minutes, gently tap the sides of the mould to release any trapped air bubbles. After about two hours a dip will form around the wicks. Pierce the wax a few times with a cocktail stick then top up with wax reheated to 82°C (180°F). Leave to set completely .

RELEASING THE CANDLE When the wax is completely cold the candle should slide easily out of the mould when the mould sealer and wick supports are removed. Snip the revealed end to about 1 cm (½ in).

DECORATING The mosaic tiles can now be stuck all around the candle using wax glue, following the manufacturer's instructions. If whole tiles do not fit around the candle accurately, use tile nippers, available from mosaics suppliers, to cut the tiles to size.

To make the lighter candle, use piping approximately 12 cm (4¾ in) in diameter and 10 cm (4 in) high. Heat up 200 g (7 oz) stearin and 1.8 kg (4 lb) of paraffin wax with approximately ⅒ of a red dye disc.

metallic ideas

The pure frosty whiteness of these sturdy pillars makes them perfect for the Christmas season, while the metallic decoration only adds to the magic. The silver and gold decoration looks like fine wire, when in fact it is actually very thin strips of flexible, self-adhesive appliqué wax. Simply cut the appliqué wax to size using a ruler and a craft knife and press it into position on the surface of the candle.

materials

5 cm (2 in) diameter wick
50 g (2 oz) stearin
450 g (16 oz) paraffin wax
metallic appliqué wax, 1 sheet to cover 1 candle

additional equipment

clear plastic pillar mould, 7 cm (2¾ in) diameter and
    18 cm (7 in) high

PREPARING THE WICK Cut the wick about 5 cm (2 in) longer than the height of the finished candle and prime it (see page 17). Use a wicking needle to thread one end of the wick through the hole at the base of the mould. Pass a cocktail stick through the wick and rest the stick across the top of the mould, holding the wick vertically down the centre. At the base of the mould pull the wick taut and seal with mould sealer.

PREPARING THE WAX Melt the stearin in a double boiler and add the paraffin wax. Continue to heat until the mixture is molten and reaches a temperature of 82°C (180°F).

FORMING THE CANDLE Pour the wax into the centre of the mould and set aside. Keep excess wax for topping up later. After a few minutes, gently tap the sides of the mould to release any trapped air bubbles. Place the filled mould in a water bath and weigh it down. After about an hour a dip will form around the wick. Pierce the wax a few times with a cocktail stick then top up with wax

reheated to 180°F (82°C). Leave to set completely.

RELEASING THE CANDLE The candle will slide easily out of the mould when the mould sealer and wick support are removed. Trim the wick at the base so that the candle stands steadily and snip the revealed end to about 1 cm (½ in).

DECORATING Metallic appliqué wax comes in ready-formed sheets of fine strips. It is quite tacky and will adhere to the surface of the candle with only gentle pressure from your fingers. To cover a whole candle, simply wrap the complete sheet around it, either vertically or horizontally and press down. You may need to trim the sheet slightly with a craft knife to achieve a snug fit. Alternatively, to cover just parts of the candle, cut off the strips with a craft knife and wrap them around the candle individually or in pairs.

To make the shorter candles simply mark a height of 15 cm (6 in) from the base of the mould on the outside of the plastic with masking tape. Use 270 g (9½ oz) of paraffin wax and 30 g (1 oz) of stearin. To make the thinner candle use a 6 cm (2⅜ in) diameter mould and mark it at a height of about 18 cm (7 in) and use the same amount of wax and stearin as above.

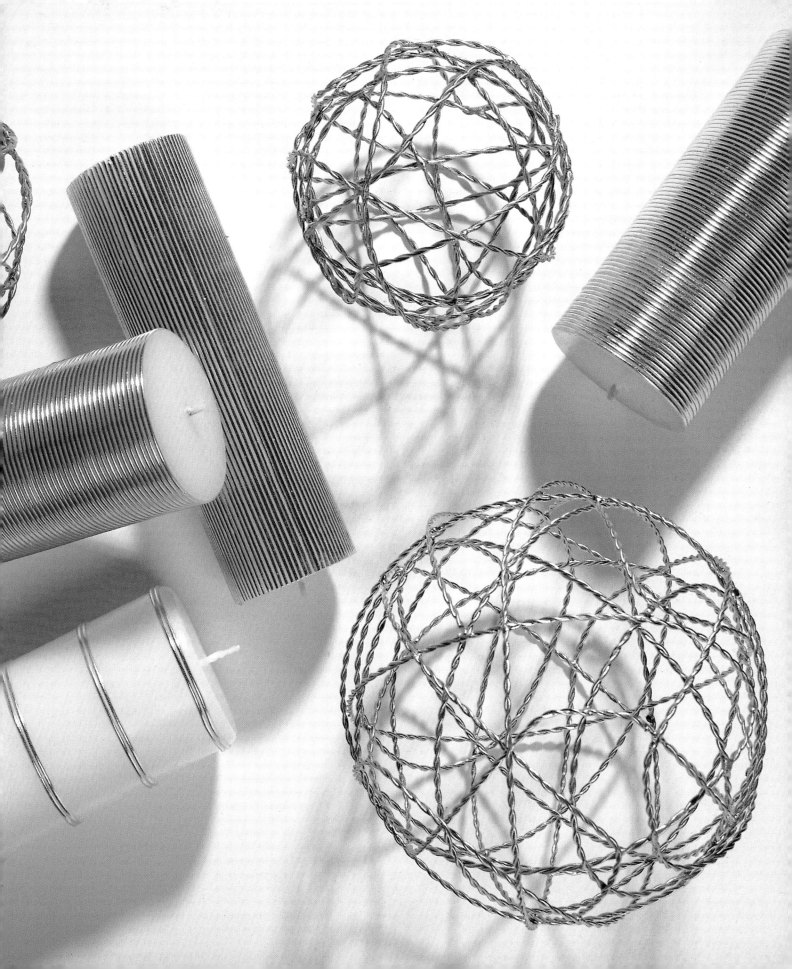

seashell square

This square candle employs a fascinating method of embedding that does not need a mould, instead walls of wax are made so that the decorative tops of seashells stick out from the wax. Other boldly coloured collected objects could also be used.

materials

selection of seashells, bought from a reputable source
4 cm (1½ in) diameter wick and a wick sustainer
900 g (31½ oz) paraffin wax
wax glue
approximately 100 g (3½ oz) stearin

additional equipment

baking tray, at least 2.5 cm (1 in) deep and about 30 cm (12 in) square (you will be making four 14 cm (5½ in) squares, so can replace one square tray with two rectangular trays)
masking tape
sharp knife

ARRANGING THE SHELLS Mark out with masking tape four 14 cm (5½ in) squares on the baking tray, leaving a small gap between each. Lay the shells, face upwards, in smaller squares within these marked squares, close to the bottom line but with a gap of 2 cm (¾ in) on either side and 4 cm (1½ in) at the top.

PREPARING THE WICK Cut the wick about 5 cm (2 in) longer than the height of the finished candle and prime it (see page 17). Attach one end to a wick sustainer.

PREPARING THE WAX The first layer of wax used does not include stearin. Melt the paraffin wax in a double boiler and continue to heat until the wax is molten and reaches a temperature of 82°C (180°F).

THE EMBEDDING TECHNIQUE Very carefully, pour a thin layer of wax into the baking tray until it covers half the height of the shells. Transfer the wax in the boiler to a bowl lined with greaseproof paper. Leave the wax on the

baking tray until it is rubbery but not completely set, then use a sharp knife to cut out the wax in the originally marked square shapes, that is, 2 cm (¾ in) on either side of the shell square and 4 cm (1½) above it. Leave the four squares of wax to set completely.

FORMING THE CANDLE SHAPE Fix the corners of the four wax "walls" together using wax glue, following the manufacturer's instructions. Place this empty wax mould on some greaseproof paper on a baking tray.

FORMING THE CANDLE Weigh out the remaining wax and calculate how much stearin you now need (10% stearin to 90% wax). Heat the stearin in the double boiler until molten, then add the paraffin wax. Reheat until molten and a temperature of 82°C (180°F). Pour a very thin layer, only up to where the shell square begins, into the centre of the wax box. After a few minutes, drop the prepared wick into the molten wax in the centre of the mould. Tie the free end around a wooden skewer and lay it across the top of the mould holding the wick vertically down the centre.

FORMING THE CANDLE Let the remaining wax cool to a temperature of no more than 65°C (150°F). It is important that the refill wax is not too hot or it will melt the embedded wax. Pour the cooled wax back into the mould in about four layers, letting the surface of each layer become rubbery before adding the next. After the final layer, keep the excess for topping up later. After about two hours a dip will form around the wick. Pierce the wax a few times with a cocktail stick then top up with wax cooled to 65°C (150°F). Leave to set completely.

FINISHING When the wax is completely cold, remove the wick support and snip the wick to 1 cm (½ in).

grain-covered pillars

Raid your kitchen cupboards for different-coloured grains to use in this project. Green pumpkin seeds, red adzuki beans and yellow and beige wheat grain are used here, but you could try orange lentils and yellow split peas that tone wonderfully with a neutral and wild rice mixture. To ring the changes, use small beads as a substitute for grains.

materials
5 cm (2 in) diameter wick
60 g (2 oz) stearin
540 g (19 oz) paraffin wax
selection of grains, here pumpkin
    seeds

additional equipment
clear plastic pillar mould, 6 cm
    (2⅜ in) diameter and 18 cm
    (7 in) high
clear plastic pillar mould 7 cm (2¾ in)
    diameter and 20 cm (8 in) high

PREPARING THE WICK Cut the wick about 5 cm (2 in) longer than the height of the finished candle and prime it (see page 17). Use a wicking needle to thread one end of the wick through the hole at the base of the first mould. Tie the free end around a wooden skewer and lay the skewer across the top of the mould holding the wick vertically down the centre. At the base of the mould pull the wick taut and seal with mould sealer.

PREPARING THE WAX Melt the stearin in a double boiler, then add the paraffin wax. Continue heating the wax until it is molten and reaches a temperature of 82°C (180°F).

FORMING THE CANDLE Pour as much of the wax as will fit into the centre of the mould, filling it to the top. Keep the excess wax for topping up and grain embellishing later. After a few minutes, gently tap the mould to release

any trapped air bubbles. After about an hour a dip will form around the wick. Pierce the wax a few times with a cocktail stick then top up with wax reheated to 82°C (180°F). Leave to set completely.

ADDING THE GRAINS When the candle is cold, remove the mould sealer and wick support and slide the candle out of the mould. Do not trim the wick yet.

Place the pillar candle inside the second plastic mould. Thread the wick through the hole in the mould and seal it with mould sealer, then attach a wick support to the other end. Pour pumpkin seeds between the sides of the two moulds to fill the gap. Remelt the remaining paraffin wax in the double boiler. When the mixture has reached 82°C (180°F), pour or spoon it into the gap between the moulds covering the seeds to a height just above the first candle. Leave to set.

FINISHING When the wax is cold the grain-covered candle will slide out of the mould easily when the mould sealer and wick support are removed. Trim the wick at the base so that the candle stands steadily and snip the revealed end to about 1 cm (½ in).

To make the red candle use a first mould 4 cm (1½ in) in diameter and 12 cm (4¾ in) high and a total of 270 g (16 oz) of paraffin wax and 30 g (1 oz) of stearin, but only fill the mould to a height of approximately 8 cm (3¼ in). Place the finished candle in a mould 5 cm (2 in) in diameter and 14 cm (5½ in) high and fill the gap with red adzuki beans and reheated wax. To make a yellow candle, embellished with beige and yellow wheat grain, use the same moulds, filled to a height of 12 cm (4¾ in) and using a total of 540 g (19 oz) of paraffin wax and 60g (2 oz) of stearin.

essential scents

Small, tapered, frosted glass containers hold delicious sorbet coloured candles, scented with fragrant essential oils. Aromatherapy is an ancient holistic practice, the benefits of which are being rediscovered and enjoyed by many today. Use the essential oils suggested on the next page, selected for their relaxing, sensual, calming and uplifting properties, or mix your own special blend, to match your mood, from the enormous selection available in chemist's and health food shops.

materials
5 cm (2 in) diameter wick and a wick sustainer
15 g (½ oz) stearin
approximately ¹⁄₁₂ of a violet dye disc
150 g (5½ oz) paraffin wax
essential oil

additional equipment
tapered square frosted glass jar, 6 cm (2⅜ in) wide at the
    base and 6 cm (2⅜ in) high

PREPARING THE WICK Cut the wick about 5 cm (2 in) longer than the height of the glass container and prime it (see page 17). Attach one end to a wick sustainer and drop the wick into the glass jar. Pass a cocktail stick through the wick and rest it across the top of the mould, holding the wick vertically down the centre.

tip

It is important to remember, when using glass containers, that the wick must be centred, since if the candle flame touches the glass it will crack or break.

PREPARING THE WAX Melt the stearin in a double boiler. Crush the violet dye with the back of a spoon. You only need this very small amount of dye to achieve a pale, delicate, sorbet colour. Add the dye to the stearin and stir to dissolve. To get an idea of the approximate finished shade, dip a strip of greaseproof paper into the dyed stearin and allow it to dry.

Add the paraffin wax and heat until the wax is molten and reaches a temperature of 82°C (180°F). Add a few drops of essential oil: the amount you add will largely depend on your own personal taste, but remember that essential oils are concentrated and only a few drops are usually needed. Stir the oil well into the wax.

FORMING THE CANDLE Pour the wax into the centre of the glass mould and keep the excess wax for topping up later. After a few minutes, gently tap the sides of the mould to release any trapped air bubbles that will distort the finished candle. After about an hour a dip will form around the wick. Pierce the wax a few times around the wick with a cocktail stick, then top up with wax reheated to 82°C (180°F), taking care not to fill above the original level of wax. Put aside to set completely.

FINISHING Remove the wick support then trim the wick to about 1 cm (½ in).

Repeat the same process to make more candles, using small amounts of pink, yellow and orange dye discs to create similar sorbet colours, and using different fragrances individually or blended together.

properties of essential oils

CITRONELLA	CAMOMILE	LAVENDER	YLANG YLANG	ROSE OIL
In addition to its wonderful revitalizing citrus aroma, citronella essential oil has insect repellent qualities ideal for balmy summer evenings outdoors.	Camomile essential oil has a distinctive smell, rather like over-ripe apples, and is well known for its calming and tranquillizing properties.	Lavender oil is a familiar fragrance to most people and is traditionally regarded as a reviving yet soothing oil. It also has antiseptic qualities.	Sensual ylang ylang essential oil is reputed to be an aphrodisiac, and is an antidepressant. It is said that in Indonesia ylang ylang flowers are spread on the bed of newly-weds on their wedding night.	Rose oil is great for calming anger, anxiety and mental tension, as well as regulating mood swings caused by premenstrual stress.

troubleshooting guide

If you follow the instructions given for each project carefully, and abide by the safety guidelines given, your candle-making experience should be pleasurable and hazard free. The resulting candles should burn beautifully, evenly and without excess smoke or spluttering. However, here are a few common problems and suggestions for how you should deal with them.

CLEANING UP: It is a good idea to cover your work surfaces and the surrounding area with newspaper, to protect against wax spills. However, in the event of spillage onto an unprotected surface, don't panic. Simply leave the wax to cool then pick or scrape it off. If it falls on fabric or upholstery, pick off as much cool wax as you can, then place brown paper over the stain and press with a hot iron. The wax will remelt and be absorbed by the paper. However, dark colours and powder dyes may leave a stain on the surface once the wax is removed.

DYES: Use powder dye sparingly since the colour is very concentrated: add only a tiny speck at a time. Remember you can always add more, but you can't take it away.

HOT WAX: Candle making is a relatively safe craft, but great care must be taken to avoid accidents when using a heat source. Never leave a double burner unattended, as the wax can ignite when heated to too high a temperature. If the wax begins to smoke it is in danger of ignition. If it does ignite, turn off the heat immediately and smother the flames with a damp tea towel or a saucepan lid. Do not try to extinguish the flame with water.

Always take care, when pouring wax, to avoid splashes. It can be a good idea to wear protective gloves.

MOULDS: Ready-made moulds must be washed in hot soapy water immediately after use. Any wax left in the mould will spoil the surface of the next candle to be cast.

When using card moulds, take care to seal all the joins carefully with packing tape to prevent seepage. Place the mould on a baking tray, so that any wax that does leak out will be caught. A little seepage may not harm the finished candle, but if a lot of wax has leaked out before the candle has set, there is nothing more you can do other than save the wax for remelting at a later date.

RELEASING THE CANDLE: If you can not remove the candle from the mould, there may not have been enough stearin in the wax mixture, meaning that the candle set too slowly, causing insufficient contraction. Place the mould in the fridge for a while then try again. If the wax had been topped up above the original level, a little of it may have seeped between the candle and the mould, making removal difficult. Place the mould in very hot water for a short while and try again.

WAX TEMPERATURE: Correct temperature is the key element to successful candle making. Use a specialist wax thermometer, or a sugar thermometer, to monitor the molten wax regularly, and pour it into the mould at the temperature indicated for each project.

For the frosted effect, it is necessary for the wax to be cooled before pouring: the scaly appearance will not work with wax that is too hot. Set the molten wax to one side and constantly monitor its cooling temperature with the thermometer. Pour into the mould at the temperature specified in the project.

When making striped candles, remember to allow each layer to cool just until the surface becomes rubbery enough to support the next layer, but not so cool as to cause separation, or so hot as to cause loss of definition.

WICKS: To ensure even burning the wick should be matched as closely as possible to the diameter of the candle. If a wick is too thick, the candle will supply insufficient fuel and the wick will burn with a large flame producing unpleasant smoke. If the wick is too thin, it will drown in the molten wax and the flame will be extinguished, or the flame will be very small.

Another important point to remember is that the wick should be centrally placed: an off-centre wick will produce lopsided burning.

templates

The following templates need to enlarged to their correct size.
To do this, photocopy each one to the percentage specified.

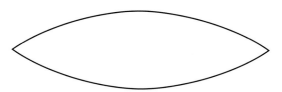

Slim Jims (see page 28) photocopy at 200%

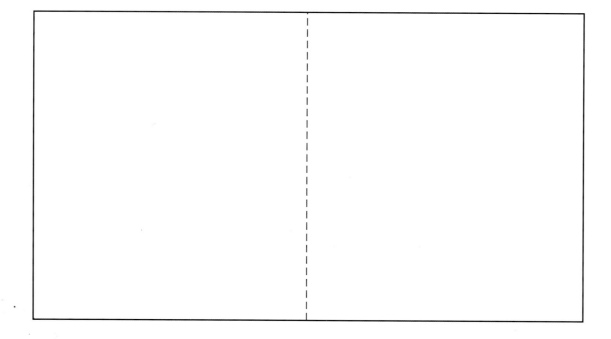

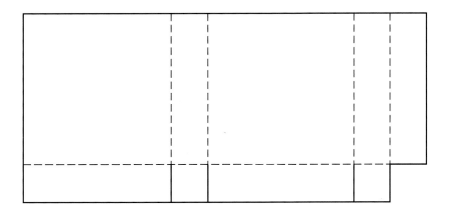

Rothko-esque (see page 50) photocopy at 400%, you will need two sheets of A3 paper

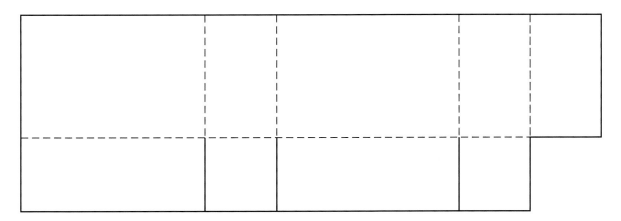

Floral Embossed, rectangle (see page 54) photocopy at 200%

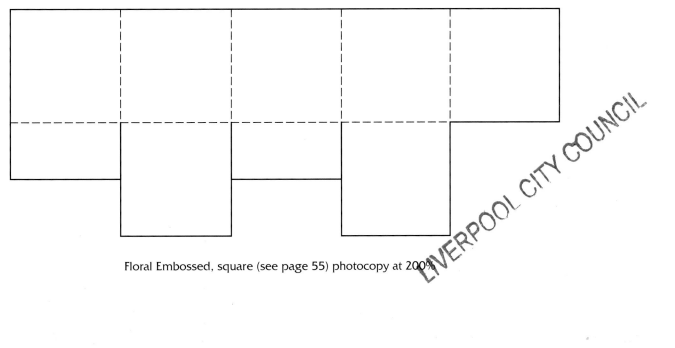

Floral Embossed, square (see page 55) photocopy at 200%

list of suppliers

UNITED KINGDOM

The Candle Shop
30 The Market
Covent Garden
London WC2E 8RE
Tel: 020 7836 9815
Fax: 020 7240 8065
Candle-making supplies

Candle Makers Supplies
28 Blythe Road
London W14 0HA
Tel: 020 7602 4031/2
Fax: 020 7602 2796
Shop and mail order candle-making supplies

Caesar Ceramics
358 Edgware Road
London W2 1EB
Tel: 020 7224 9671
Fax: 020 7224 9854
For mirror mosaic tiles

Homecrafts Direct
PO Box 38
Leicester LE1 9BU
Tel: 0116 251 3139
Mail order candle-making supplies

Panduro Hobby
Westway House
Transport Avenue
Brentford
Middlesex TW8 9HF
Tel: 020 8847 6161
Fax: 020 8847 5073
Orders: 01392 427788
Mail order catalogue

Senses Candle Design
5G Atlas Business Centre
Oxgate Lane

Staples Corner
London NW2 7HJ
Tel/Fax: 020 8450 3255
Candles and candle-making supplies

E.H. Thorne Ltd
Beehive Works
Wragby
Lincoln LN3 5LA
Tel: 01673 858555
Fax: 01673 857004
Website: www.thorne.co.uk
Mail order beeswax and candle-making supplies

INTERNET RESOURCES

www.waxworkshop.demon.co.uk
Candles, accessories, kits

www.wicksend.co.uk
Candles and candleholders

SOUTH AFRICA

Art, Craft & Hobbies
72 Hibernia Street
George 6529
Tel/Fax: (0448) 74 1337

Artwise
337 Sanlam Centre
King's Road
Pinetown
Durban 3610
Tel: (031) 701 1824

Crafty Suppliers
Shop 104
Upper Ground Level
The Atrium, Claremont
Cape Town 7700
Tel: (021) 671 0286

Yours Forever Home Craft Studio
92 Heritage Market
Hillcrest 3610
Tel: (031) 765 6769

Southern Arts & Crafts
105 Main Street
Rosettenville
Johannesburg 2130
Tel/Fax: (011) 683 6566

AUSTRALIA

Arts and Craft Centre
34 Mint Street
East Victoria Park, WA 6101
Tel: (08) 9361 4567

Candle Creations
9 Francis Road
Wingfield, SA 5013
Tel: (08) 8347 2525

The Candle Factory
80 George Street, NSW 2000
Tel: (02) 9241 3365

Candles Galore
11 Campbell Terrace
Alderley, Brisbane 4055
Tel: 1800 819 792

The Craft Company
272 Victoria Avenue
Chatswood, NSW 2067
Tel: (02) 413 1718

Gift Ware Agencies
Unit 207 West Point Centre
396 Scarborough Road
Osborne Park, WA 6017
Tel: (08) 9246 9445

Hornsby Beekeeping Supplies
63A Hunter Street
Hornsby, NSW 2077
Tel: (02) 477 5569

Janet's Art Supplies
145 Victoria Avenue
Cahatswood, NSW 2067
Tel: (02) 417 8527

Mr Craft
Coolung Lane
Eastwood, NSW 2122
Tel: (02) 858 2868

Pacific Petroleum Products
1495 Warrego Highway
Ipswich, QLD 4305
Tel: (07) 3201 7566

Stacks of Wax
239 Australia Street
Newtown, NSW 2142
Tel: (02) 9660 0017

The Wizard of the Wick Candle Co.
1/584 Waterworks Road
Ashgrove, QLD 4060
Tel: (07) 3366 7003

or write to:
PO Box 2129
West Ashgrove, QLD 4060
Candle-making classes

NEW ZEALAND

Aglow Wax & Wix
Box 7000
Auckland
Tel: (09) 834 6000

Golding Handcrafts
PO Box 9022
Wellington
Tel/Fax: (04) 801 5855
Web: www.goldingcraft.com

Handcraft Supplies NZ Ltd
13-19 Rosebank Road
Avondale
Auckland
Tel: (09) 828 9834

National Candles Ltd
128 Egmont Street
PO Box 6024
Wellington
Tel: (04) 384 6806
Fax: (04) 384 7500

Waxglo House
1013 Ferry Road
Woolston
PO Box 19800
Christchurch
Tel: (03) 384 4188
Fax: (03) 384 4777

UNITED STATES

Barker Enterprises Inc.
15106 10th Avenue
SW Seattle
WA 98166
Tel: (206) 244 1870

Candlestick
2444 Broadway
New York
NY 10024
Tel: (212) 787 5444

Dick Blick
PO Box 1267
Galesburg
IL 61402
Tel: (309) 343 6181

General Wax and Candle Co.
6863 Beck Avenue
North Hollywood
CA 91605
Tel: (800) 929 7867

Pottery Barn
Mail Order Department
PO Box 7044
San Francisco
CA 91420–7044
Tel: (800) 922 5507

Pourette Candle Making Supplies
1418 NW 53rd St
PO Box 17056
Seattle
WA 98107
Tel: (880) 888 wick

Yankee Candle Company
PO Box 110
South Deerfield
MA 01373
Tel: (800) 243 1776

CANADA

Charlotte Hobbys
782 Shield Road
Hemmingford
Quebec J0I IH0
Tel: (516) 247 2590

Lynden House International Inc.
12605A 127 Avenue
Edmonton
Alberta T5L 3E8
Tel: (780) 448 1994

Further Reading

The New Candle Book, Gloria
Nicol, Lorenz Books

Inspirations Candles, Diana Civil,
Lorenz Books

Candle Making in a Weekend,
Sue Spear, New Holland

index